American Cultural Patterns:
A Cross-Cultural Perspective

Edward C. Stewart

intercultural press inc.

INTERCULTURAL PRESS
P.O. Box 768
Yarmouth, Maine 04096

Library of Congress Catalogue No. 70-26361

ISBN 0-933662-01-7

Printed in the United States of America
Thirteenth Printing 1985

Ronald C. Howard

PREFACE

This book was originally written by Edward Stewart when he was with the Human Relations Resource Office at George Washington University in Washington, D.C. It was revised during the time he was a Research Professor with the Graduate School of Public and International Affairs at the University of Pittsburgh (1966-69) and further revised since then. Thus it is the end product of a long process of thought, research and practical experimentation.

For Americans, Dr. Stewart's book provides a solid and, for many, a new cross-cultural perspective on their own beliefs and behavior. In it he speaks directly to the questions many Americans concerned with cross-cultural relations or intercultural communications must answer. It is hoped that it will also contribute to the growing crystallization of cross-cultural psychology and intercultural communication as fields of study.

Dr. Stewart was born in Sao Paolo, Brazil, and came to the U.S. as a boy. He served in the U.S. Army in Europe during the Second World War and later took his Ph.D. in Psychology at the University of Texas. He has taught at Lehigh University in the areas of perception theory and social psychology. In 1959 he joined the Human Resources Research Office at the George Washington University and in 1962 began to work principally in the area of intercultural communication. He has continued his research and teaching specialization in this area since then, working successively at the University of Pittsburgh, the University of Delaware, the Peace Corps, the Washington International Center, and the University of Southern California's Washington Education Center.

Dr. Stewart has served as a consultant on intercultural communication with the Peace Corps, the Agency for International Development, the Foreign Service Institute, the Military Assistance Institute, the Business Council for International Understanding, the American University, the Regional Council for International Education, Westinghouse Corporation, the DuPont Corporation, and a number of other training, business and governmental organizations. He has made a major contribution to the field of cross-cultural training by developing a simulation exercise using non-American actors to role-play "contrast-Americans" in scenarios based on the overseas experiences of technical advisors. He has also published a variety of reports and papers in this field.

David S. Hoopes
President
Intercultural Network, Inc.

TABLE OF CONTENTS

AUTHOR'S INTRODUCTION

The objective of this report is to supply a perspective on some of the cross-cultural problems encountered by American advisors, academicians and technicians overseas or by Americans such as foreign student advisors working in an intercultural milieu in the United States. The approach has been to formulate the cross-cultural problems as differences between patterns of thinking, assumptions and values held by such Americans and those held by the foreigners with whom they work. These cultural differences often produce misunderstandings and lead to ineffectual activity in face-to-face communications. A concerted effort on the part of Americans to understand them would probably enhance their effectivenss overseas and in the United States. It is postulated, however, that achievement of this goal would require that the advisors first know American culture. Since the typical American lacks a clear understanding of his own culture, there is a need for a delineation of the patterns of thinking, assumptions and values that frequently affect advising and consulting activities overseas and at home.

Although a critical examination of obstacles to cross-cultural communication suggests, in many instances, how Americans should act, it is not our objective here to prescribe behavior. The purpose, rather, is to present schematic descriptions of some important aspects of American culture and to show some of their consequences for cross-cultural communication.

The report is intended not only for foreign student advisors and for Americans working or training to work overseas, but also for instructors and trainers of AID technicians, Peace Corps volunteers, and others concerned with problems of cultural change. Gearing the treatment thus to operational needs has resulted in the deliberate skirting of numerous issues concerning the meaning of "culture," "values," and other matters of interest primarily to the social science scholar rather than the practitioner.

In the first chapter the cross-cultural problems encountered by American advisors and consultants are described briefly and in general terms. Brief mention is made, also, of the sources used in developing the description and conceptualization of American culture. In chapter 2 of Part I the concepts **patterns of thinking**, **assumptions** and **values** are discussed with a view to dispelling the confusion which has surrounded the uses of these terms. In particular, a distinction is made between assumptions and values which have reference to actual behavior, and those which are invoked "ritualistically" (frequently for emotional reasons) and which often fail to describe the real actions of the individual. The term **cultural norms** will be used to classify the latter.

In Part III substantive descriptions of American assumptions and values are provided. Each chapter in this section deals with one of the following topics (which may be seen as the individual components of a cultural pattern or system of assumptions and values): form of activity, form of relation to others, perception of the world and perception of the self. These components approximate continuous dimensions (rather than discrete categories), in terms of which any given culture may be represented. It is important to note that within the same culture several variations of the same component normally occur. Despite this variety, each culture is usually typified by a dominant form of each component. In American culture those values commonly associated with the American middle-class are seen as dominant. Clearly, however, these do not encompass all the significant values and value systems shared by large numbers of Americans.

The theme of relativity of assumptions and values is stressed throughout the report by presenting American cultural characteristics in conjunction with variations from other cultures or from American culture itself.

The final section, Part IV, records some of the consequences of the cultural differences in the face-to-face interaction between Americans and their counterparts.

An effort has been made throughout this report to employ the concepts most familiar to trainees, students, and advisors. The language and concepts of social scientists have been avoided as far as possible when they do not have familiar connotations. But what is hoped to be a practical gain represents a sacrifice in theoretical coherence. Specifically, the writer has relied extensively upon the work of Florence R. Kluckhohn without, however, adopting her complete system of theoretical concepts. The writer assumes responsibility for misrepresentations which may appear as a result.

The influence of George M. Foster is also pervasive throughout parts of this report. His work, and that of Robin M. Williams, Jr., have been freely used, but the interpretations made are the responsibility of this writer.

Florence Kluckhohn, George Foster and Robin Williams, Jr., have provided substantive comments on an original draft. The writer is indebted to them for their incisiveness, kindness and patience in reviewing and is apologetic to Florence Kluckhohn and George Foster, in particular, for distorting their writings to fit the mold of specific objectives.

Part I
CONCEPTUALIZATION
OF THE PROBLEM

Success or failure in counseling foreign students in the United States or in providing technical assistance overseas rests ultimately upon the ability of the American advisor to influence the behavior of his associates.* Although there are other ways of considering the problem of counseling and of giving technical assistance, at some stage of the process the American must act in the capacity of an advisor to the foreign associates with whom he is working and relinquish the role of an expert or technician. The requirements placed on the American as an advisor have been chosen as the focus of this report; hence the stress is on the interpersonal relations between the American consultant and his associates. This point of view does not deny the importance of language ability, technical competence, and administrative skill, but it does hold that interpersonal relations comprise an important aspect of most cross-cultural programs in the United States and overseas and provide a better guide to understanding their results.

1. THE CROSS-CULTURAL PROBLEM

Sources of Information

Since little systematic attention has been given to the effects of sociocultural factors on interpersonal relations, behavioral guides supported by cross-cultural research are not available for the advisor overseas (Lundstedt, 1961, 375). Most of the information contained in the literature is peripheral to interpersonal relations since the stress is on customs, values and culture. These books and articles have been written by anthropologists and other social scientists, as well as by travelers, and persons who have worked overseas. Many of them are anecdotal; only a few are analytical. Some are evaluative, and these come closest to considering interpersonal relations in a cross-cultural setting.** Typically, however, little attention is given to how cultural concepts can be employed systematically to describe the behavior of **individual** Americans working with foreign persons. This literature has been useful, nevertheless.

---

*The terms advisor, consultant, and technician are used interchangeably to refer to Americans whose primary function is to make their experience, skills, and judgment available to their foreign associates, and for whom administration or actual implementation is either secondary or nonexistent. The foreigners with whom the Americans work are referred to as either counterparts, associates or co-workers.

See Arensberg and Niehoff, 1964; Cleveland, **et al., 1960; Erasmus, 1961; Foster, 1962.

A second source of information used has been interviews with AID technicians, Peace Corps volunteers and military advisors. All of them have provided information on cross-cultural problems in their own particular realms. They did not, however, use a coherent psychological frame of reference to integrate their information; for this and other reasons it is difficult to separate opinion from fact, or to determine the generality of their observations. The collections of facts, anecdotes, and generalizations they provided serve to illustrate aspects of working cross-culturally, but this raw material needs to be conceptualized. The subjectivity must be removed and the information generalized and abstracted in a coherent frame of reference.

These sources have been augmented by the writer's own observations abroad.

The purpose now is to relate the basic elements of culture to interpersonal dimensions relevant to cross-cultural cooperation. The objective is to describe those American cultural characteristics which are inherent in the behavior of American advisors in their interpersonal relations with foreigners, either in the United States or abroad, with whom they are working. This goal requires the assumption that counseling programs in this country and projects overseas contain common features, and, also, that most countries to which Americans are sent present common issues to the advisors. Both of these factors are briefly considered below.

Common Characteristics of Non-Western Countries

The American advisor usually goes to non-Western or developing countries, mostly in Africa, Asia, and Latin America. Each of these countries differs from the others in some respects, but as former colonies or territories within the spheres of influence of European countries or Great Britain, they exhibit many common characteristics vis-a-vis the industrialized West. The existence of similarities among non-Western countries does not imply, however, that cultures throughout the world can be depicted along a single dimension with the industrial West at one end and the non-West at the other. Many exceptions will be found to the general contrast provided between American culture (characterized as an extreme development of urban society) and non-Western cultures. For example, the Thailander is a member of a culture which is usually described as rural and traditional, or **gemeinschaft**. One of the characteristics ordinarily found in this kind of culture is that the individual defines himself in terms of social links — more usually obligations — with members of his immediate family and extended group. The Thai, however, usually does not show this characteristic, since he typically conceives of himself as an autonomous individual. In this respect his self concept is very similar to that of a middle-class American who is a member of a **gesellschaft** culture, a term applied to the technologically developed West. On the other hand, the Japanese, who — like the American — is a member of a highly industrialized nation, defines himself in terms of a system of social links with his family and extended group. In this context the implications of the various definitions of the self are two-fold: a given aspect of the culture of a non-Western country may sometimes be more similar to a corresponding feature of Western culture than to that of other non-Western countries; and secondly, industrialization does not necessarily assume the pattern found in the United States.

The contrast between American culture and the culture of non-Western nations is further complicated by variations within each culture. Not all members of a culture are the same. There may be more cultural variation within a culture than between the dominant aspects of two separate cultures. Any description of a society that does not accommodate cultural variations is out of joint. The task of drawing a contrast between two societies or two groups of societies, however, is not as hopeless as it may first appear. Florence Kluckhohn asserts that all human beings, irrespective of background or conditions of life, face a limited number of common human problems — such as are involved in man's relation to nature or which are innate human nature (F. Kluckhohn, 1963, 221-222). The number of possible solutions to these universal human problems is limited. In each society are found the full range of possible solutions to them, but a dominant solution is usually present with alternative solutions existing as cultural variations (see F. Kluckhohn, 1963, 221).

A description of differences between cultures, which takes into account variations **within** cultures, can be accomplished by using dimensions rather than categories as systematic terms of exposition. The dimensions employed have much in common with the value orientations used by Florence Kluckhohn. They will be used as a bridge to other cultures which provide contrasting examples to American culture. As with American society, the foreign ones will be considered primarily in terms of their dominant cultural patterns.

In looking at the dominant patterns of cultures throughout the world, it is found that American culture usually lies at one end of the dimensions and the cultures of non-Western nations occupy positions proceeding in the opposite direction. For example, the Iranian, the Ecuadorian, and the Chinese on Taiwan differ in the qualities which they value in person, but in comparison with middle-class Americans, the members of each of these societies place more stress on family and position in society. In the United States, individual achievement is usually valued above family relationships. In this respect (and in many if not most others—as far as cultural assumptions and values are concerned) the American middle-class differs from most non-Western culture groups. It is legitimate, therefore, to compare people of the non-Western countries with Americans even though the non-Western countries themselves differ markedly.

Cultural Aspects of Overseas Missions

In the same way that the underdeveloped countries have a number of shared characteristics, the many jobs which Americans perform overseas present similar aspects. The American is supposed to consult or advise, and not to perform work; thus his goals are usually less tangible and concrete than those to which he is accustomed. If work and social position are not clearly structured, the individual is thrown back upon his own resources in making decisions, evaluating situations, and pursuing courses of action. Routine matters then become major problems. Cultural differences pervade inter-personal relations. As a consequence the American's work is affected since the cultural differences between himself and his counterpart become intensified and assume significance. In the same manner that the American may not have cultural support for his work, he may also be deprived of the social support afforded by working within a familiar organization. He is either isolated or else absorbed into a foreign social structure. He does not carry with him his own working environment. Customary services and even the advice or moral support provided by colleagues will often be missing.

Many Americans find when they arrive overseas that their work assumes a character quite different from what they were led to expect. A training problem takes on a new aspect for the advisor when he learns, for example, that in addition to speaking only their native language, his trainees are illiterate. Sometimes the health program does not get off the ground because the people do not have the concept of germs and therefore do not understand preventive health measures and — most upsetting of all — their culture provides an explanation of disease and health incompatible with Western scientific discoveries. In short, what is aptly labeled "training," "education," "health," in the United States may acquire an entirely different character overseas. A particularly disturbing problem faced by the advisor may be the intransigence of local officials and government, so that his job becomes a task of persuading and influencing his counterpart and associates. The advisor is sometimes compelled to accept, perhaps bitterly, the frustration of his objectives. One of the undesirable consequences of such an eventuality is that the American, having been deprived of concrete achievements, may develop a feeling of failure. This attitude is often compounded by the realization that his services are not wanted. (This has been particularly true of the military advisors and usually untrue of the Peace Corps volunteer.) He is accepted as a necessary evil since he brings with him materiel and prestige, but his advice is not always welcomed.

Americans overseas readily observe and describe cross-cultural differences of language, customs and preferences. The fact that these differences may be easily perceived often obscures the deeply imbedded but more profound disparities in concepts about the world and experience and in patterns of thought and modes of action, all of which affect the person-to-person interaction of the advisor and his counterpart. Slight differences in the behavior, thoughts and emotions of their associates may not always be perceived by Americans, but as they produce a cumulative effect they require an interpretation, and the explanation most likely to occur to the advisor is bias, either personal or cultural. The counterpart often appears as a man who opposes the advisor either as a person or as an American, or, perhaps, simply as an advisor. Contributing to this reaction and sometimes giving it substance is the fact that the American's co-workers are likely to have a stereotype of Americans. Slight American traits or nontypical American behavior may suggest gangster or millionaire, sexual promiscuity, peanut butter, or the Twist. The American stereotype may have originated with Americans known previously. It may also have been built up by hearsay and through the media of mass communication. Aspects of the stereotype may run counter to the American's emotional and cultural standards of reference. For instance, "Yankee" no longer means "New Englander"; it also includes the Southerner, the Westerner, and the Negro. The heightened meaning and effect of nationalism abroad takes on added significance when the American, as in the case of most advisors, is a representative of the government.

Cultural Aspects of Counseling Foreign Students

Many of the problems faced by the American advisor overseas are encountered in reverse by the foreign student arriving in the United States. He may already be uncertain about his life and education in his university. American correspondence is notoriously ambiguous from the foreigner's point of view. Offers to assist the student when he arrives are often literally interpreted to mean that arrangements for living accommodations have been made and that the student will be met upon arrival. He is disappointed to discover that he may have to search for a room or apartment, selecting from a list of addresses obtained from the university. The African student in particular may be unprepared to understand how the university will send him to an address where he is told that the "room has just been rented," though it obviously has not.

· Although the diversity of abilities, interests and backgrounds of foreign students is enormous, there are general attitudes and problems. Many foreign students hold in awe American technology, science and business. They believe that in American culture there are "methods" in these fields which they should master. The foreign students often have a sense of inferiority in material things, in science and methodology which is mitigated by a feeling of cultural superiority. Americans are percieved to lack values and culture, to turn their backs on history, custom and tradition which for the foreign student are the sources of culture. Americans are concerned with progress which means technology and materialism and so is the foreign student, but he wishes for progress without relinquishing his own cultural values.

Americans are likely to generalize to all foreigners certain American characteristics of human relations which are considered universal. The foreigner is either ignored or he is treated with great care, bordering on condescension. The foreign student may miss the resilience and commitment in human relations to which he is accustomed. He finds it easy to be included in social and academic groups but difficult to be accepted into the inner circles. In many cases he may be searching for an intimacy and closeness in social relations which is largely absent from American social and academic life. Eventually the foreign student may master the language and customs of American social relations which are then used with a severity that exposes their ambiguity. While he may see American ways as hypocritical, the foreign student, being unable to perceive the nuances of American life, may be seen as crude and inconsiderate.

In the academic world itself, the American instructor may have expecta-tions of the foreign students which the latter find difficult to accept. For instance, the participatory atmosphere and relative equality of the classroom is unusual for most foreign students. If a student attempts to deviate from his own educational traditions and participates actively in the classroom, he may over-react, monopolizing too much time and speaking dogmatically. To his instructor, he now appears arrogant and domineering.

Many foreign students may master the jargon and stereotypes of thinking in their academic field. In the areas of education and of the social sciences, for example, the student may learn to sprinkle his conversation with terms such as "analytical thinking," "decision-making," "model," "problem-solving," and "dependent variables." The instructor may react with discomfort at the liberality with which his favorite jargon is used in places where he himself would not employ it. Unable to make the same discriminating judgment as the instructor, the student betrays the cultural underpinning of much of the jargon and thought in the academic world. The instructor, however, is not likely to be aware of the cultural involution of his thought and language, preferring to attribute it to scholarship or to science. As a consequence he often decides that the foreign student is incapable of thinking analytically, a conclusion which is not necessarily justified.

Turning to the foreign student advisor, we encounter a person who is immersed in his own culture in the same way as any other American. His effectiveness in working with foreign students resides in his ability to attain an attitude of cultural relativity towards American culture and perceptivity to other cultures. The foreign student advisor is effective if he is able to diagnose the problems of the foreign students by separating those caused by cultural differences from those originating in personality traits of the students. The advisor should also be able to identify problems precipitated by a clash between the personal objectives of the students and the legitimate aims of the school. It is important for the foreign student advisor to become familiar with the experience of foreign students who feel that the educational institution or the host culture makes blind impositions upon them. The students almost inevitably become hyper-reactive. Because they periodically require occasions to ventilate their feelings, they need opportunities to be with people who demonstrate respect for values, ways of thinking, and styles of living other than their own.

Foreign student advisors frequently conduct programs seeking to broaden relations among American and foreign students. Unfortunately these enterprises comprise one of their least effective activities. They make the typical American assumption that bringing people together in some form of social activity will spontaneously produce meaningful cross-cultural interactions. Experience negates the assumption and reveals the need for the advisor to possess awareness of his own cultural and social predispositions.

The average American college student tends to embody thoroughly the American value system. Unless American students, or particular groups within the American student body, can be helped to recognize the unconscious assumptions they make and insist upon in others, unless they can be stimulated to work at establishing genuine cross-cultural relationships, the foreign student may be compelled either to retreat into an enclave of foreign or compatriot students or to discard his own culture and become "Americanized." The psychological implications for the student of either of these alternatives are serious and often detrimental to effective adjustment or the attainment of his educatonal aims while in this country.

It is therefore the responsibility of the foreign student advisor to assume an educational role toward the American students on his campus. It is here, of course, that the great opportunity lies in having students from other countries on the campus—to enhance the quality of the education for Americans. There is thus a reciprocal relationship established. As the American student contributes to the adjustment of the foreign student he is able to broaden his perspectives and learn about himself. As the foreign student helps his

American colleague to grow and expand his horizons, he serves some of his own needs for adjustment to American culture.

2. CULTURAL DIFFERENCES

Patterns of Perception

The world of perception presents an incredibly rich experience of stimulation. It has been estimated that vision alone confronts the human eye with 7,500,000 distinguishable colors (Geldard, 1953, 53). If to colors are added other dimensions of vision such as perception of form, lightness and space, the perceptual world emerges as a potential array of bewildering stimulation. Although vision may be the richest of the senses, hearing itself has been estimated to provide approximately 340,000 discriminable tones (Geldard, 1953, 124). Smell, touch, kinesthesis, pain, taste, and the other remaining senses contribute to a richness of perceptual experience that lies beyond the province of understanding as well as imagination.

Perceptual stimulation does not necessarily predict the responses of the individual and behavior does not necessarily reveal the external environment. An understanding of the relation between perception and behavior requires the elaboration of an intervening stage of the "perceiver" since it is a repeated finding that perceptual responses are influenced by the individual's expectations. To an extent not usually recognized, perception resides in the perceiver and not in the external world. The expectation of the perceiver endows the visual dimensions of perception—the qualities of color, shape, brightness and others—with meaning so that what is perceived is objects such as persons, animals, trees and landscapes. The process of perception is concerned with objects perceived according to the expectations of the individual so that even the most immediate and simple perception reveals the perceiver as well as the perceived.

In acquiring the patterns of thinking, values and assumptions which represent culture, the perceiver learns to categorize perceptual stimulation and reduces the overwhelming complexity of the sensory world. In effect, the perceiver does not respond to a specific stimulus, a shade of blue, for instance; but, instead, responds to a "blue" or a "red" perceived as a category containing many discriminable colors. Since the categories of stimulation underlying perceptual responses are learned by the perceiver, they can be associated with his personal and cultural background.

It can be shown, for instance, that the ability to discriminate colors improves with possession of the vocabulary for labeling the color perceived. In the absence of labels, discrimination is poorer. It can also be shown that the categories for classifying colors vary for different groups or cultures. In some societies, the distinctions between warm and cold colors may be emphasized, leading to impoverished discriminability between colors such as blue and green.

The observations on the perceptions of colors contradict the traditional view that the perceiver confronts a specific, objective and physical reality. Instead, the conclusion asserts that the perceiver responds to a class of stimuli rather than to a particular stimulus. The process of categorization produces images and concepts which classify things and provide a means of coping with the complexity of the perceptual world. "To categorize is to render discriminably different things equivalent, to group the objects and events and people around us into classes, and to respond to them in terms of their class membership rather than their uniqueness" (Bruner **et al**., 1956, 1).

The perceptual diversity found among people throughout different societies remains exotic information until categorization or abstraction is seen to underlie both perception and thinking. Then the process of thinking itself can be considered to differ according to the effects of culture in the same manner that perception does. Some would say that there is no basic difference between "what happens when a person looks at the world directly and when he sits with his eyes closed and thinks" (Arnheim, 1969, 133). Culture will affect thinking as it affects perception if both processes are considered to be governed by the same principles. There is a style of thinking referred to as associative (Glenn, 1966) or relational (Cohen, 1969) which parallels the perceptual process and hence strengthens the view that perception and thinking are continuous.

A more conservative view stresses the continuity between perception and thinking and at the same time emphasizes the predominance of sensory components in perception, "while in thinking, central components predominate" (Helson, 1964, 457). Some patterns of thinking are relatively remote from the world of images and perceptual responses; Glenn refers to them as **abstract** and Cohen as **analytical** (Cohen, 1969). They are characterized by abstract concepts which are used to analyze the world into categories which have no apparent perceptual representation.

Assumptions and Values

The typical person has a strong sense of what the world is really like, so that it is with surprise that he discovers that "reality" is built up out of certain assumptions commonly shared among members of the same culture. Cultural assumptions may be defined as abstract, organized and general concepts which pervade a person's outlook and behavior. These same properties of assumptions are not characteristic of behavior, which is concrete, discrete and specific.

Members of different cultures possess various ideas of reality since their assumptions about both the world and experience differ. Most Americans, for instance, implicitly assume the world external to themselves and to others is physical, material, and does not have a soul or a spirit. The truth of these assumptions may appear to be self-evident but, in fact, they are not shared by many peoples throughout the non-Western world. Large segments of the peoples throughout South- and Southeast Asia endow nature with an essence similar to the one reserved for man by Westerners. It is this assumption which, in part, predisposes Westerners and Americans in particular to exploit the physical environment to their own purposes. Conversely, the Indian or the Southeast Asian finds himself attempting to synthesize or integrate with nature because he assumes that this is the relationship naturally existing. Man is just another form of life and does not possess unique attributes which set him apart from other forms or even from topographical features of the environment such as a mountain or a valley.

Basic assumptions, such as the perception of the self and the perception of the world, can be inferred from actions of an individual; however, several assumptions are usually required to explain fully any particular behavior. Furthermore, these basic perceptions do not inevitably fix the direction in which an individual acts. For example, the middle-class American usually thinks of himself as an individual, the world as inanimate, success as his goal, impersonal cooperation with others as desirable, and **doing** as his preferred activity. Do these assumptions mean that he should become a businessman or a social worker? Should he take an active part in local politics or does he confine his political activity to the voting booth? Does he engage in discussion by outlining the main issues before proceeding to details and applications or does he follow the reverse direction? All of these questions are related to the basic assumptions of the individual and reflect the cultural pattern of American middle-class society. They do not, however, completely govern the actions of the individual. Most decisions, actions and evaluations are considered according to concepts less abstract, less generalized and less organized than the cultural assumptions. For example, most Americans assume that nature is material and exploitable and this assumption is related to the fact that Americans usually desire material comfort and possessions. People should have shelter, clothing, warmth and all of the other means that make the individual materially comfortable. It is also desirable and acceptable that the individual have his own car, house and other physical possessions. If an American were to give away all of his possessions, deny himself material comforts and choose to dress in rags while wandering in the pursuit of spiritual grace, his actions would be more in keeping with the cultural patterns of parts of Asia. In the United States the individual's behavior would probably be considered as a deviation from the pursuit of material comfort and possessions. Whatever reasons the individual might advance for pursuing the Biblical road to salvation would usually be considered eccentric, for most Americans do not recognize incompatibility between the goal of acquiring material comfort and possessions and that of leading a good life.

Although everyone knows Americans who are not particularly concerned with physical comfort, it is apparent that material comfort is the dominant pattern when one notes the time, effort and money expended by Americans on labor-saving devices, comfortable means of transportation, etc. In India on the other hand, the stress on spiritual grace rather than on material comfort is readily observed. The fundamental difference between the two cultures (or any cultures) is the difference in the stress given each possible set of assumptions and actions.

We shall call **values** those concepts such as the desirability of material comfort and possessions. The choice of this term is made on the basis of its simplicity and common usage and in the face of considerable ambiguities attending its theoretical use (see F. Kluckhohn and F. Strodtbeck, 1961; C. Kluckhohn, 1951). The concept of **value** has been employed in many different ways. In one comprehensive review of the subject, the writer concludes that the one feature that is common to all usages is the idea of **oughtness**, (C. Kluckhohn, 1951, 388-433) and this is the definition adopted here. Explicitly avoided is use of the term value to connote those preferences or choices of the individual illustrated by choices in foods, cars, magazines, etc. To include this meaning under value would make the concept too encompassing to have utility, since all human choices would then be dependent on value. It is well to point out, however, the distinctions among preferences, values, and assumptions are not sharp. These concepts are connected, one merging into the other. Furthermore, what is a preference for one person may be a value for another and both, of course, will be associated with assumptions.

Cultural Dimensions and Diversities

In contrasting American culture with those of the non-Western nations, we will find that in most instances American middle-class culture will provide one end of a continuum, whereas the opposite end will be derived from various other cultures. In this manner, by the use of at least two examples, it is hoped that a basic dimension will be presented in which any culture or variation of a culture can be depicted. For instance, when Americans are described as assuming that the world is physical and material, it is implied that this view is at one end of a dimension running from the physical, material world, to a world in which all nature has life and an essence similar to the "soul" or "humanness" that Westerners attribute only to man himself. According to this view, typical of many Indians, the world is not qualitatively different from man; both are forms made of the same stuff and both are animated by the same forces. A continuum is implied also in the areas of values and patterns of thinking. The American stress on material comforts, for example, is opposed to the Oriental value on the state of grace of the individual.

Conceiving of patterns of thinking, assumptions and values as lying along linear dimensions often presents an over-simplification. Sometimes opposite pairs of cultural phenomena may seem ambiguous, since the polar terms will be related along complex dimensions. The concept of dimensions will be sustained in drawing attention to both the dominant characteristics of a culture and the variant patterns. The importance of diversity of patterns of thinking, assumptions and values within the same society should not be overlooked. F. Kluckhohn has written that:

> ...in most of the analyses of the common value element in culture patterning, the dominant values of peoples have been overstressed and **variant** values largely ignored... Our most basic assumption is that there is a **systematic variation** in the realm of cultural phenomena which is both as definite and as essential as the demonstrated systematic variation in physical and biological phenomena.
>
> The varying types of life activities which are essential to the functions of a social system are an obvious source of both a **required** and a **permitted** variation within the system (F. Kluckhohn and Strodtbeck, 1961, 3).

Anthony Wallace also stressed diversity within the same culture (Wallace, 1961, 21-41). He presents an ingenious argument which shows how two individuals from the same culture are much more likely to have diverse rather than uniform outlooks. Using the term **cognitive map** as roughly synonymous with patterns of thinking, assumptions and values, Wallace states that:

...Ritual, for instance, is often differently conceptualized by viewers and performers; public entertainment similarly is variously perceived by professional and audience; the doctor (or shaman) and patient relationship demands a mutual understanding. Even in class and political relationships, complementary roles (as for instance, between the holders of "Great" and "Little" Traditions) are notoriously difficult of exchange. Administrative personnel and leaders generaliy must understand the system on a "higher" level of synthesis than their subordinates, a level which demands a different because more abstract, cognitive map. Indeed, we now suggest that human societies may characteristically **require** the non-sharing of certain cognitive maps among participants in a variety of institutional arrangements (Wallace, 1961, 39-40).

The scope of this book requires a deliberate focus upon the dominant pattern of middle-class Americans. Variant patterns will be introduced only for the purpose of avoiding too great a distortion of American society. In finding contrasting examples from other societies we shall again turn to the dominant regularities, rather than to cultural variations. We will not be able to do full justice to the rich diversities found in American middle-class society or in the cultures of the non-West.

Values and Cultural Norms

Values, as we will use the term, as well as assumptions, are systematic concepts which can be used to describe behavior. Some values which we will call **cultural norms** are explicit and are repeatedly invoked by Americans to describe or justify their actions. Because cultural norms are related to behavior as cliches, rituals or as cultural platitudes, they provide inaccurate descriptions of behavior. Americans, for instance, quite often extol the virtues of self-reliance;* they think of themselves as self-reliant and are so perceived by others. At the same time they accept social security, borrow money, and in innumerable ways show willingness to depend on others to various extents. "Self-reliance" as a value has an emotional impact upon Americans and hence affects their actions but it does not provide a systematic explanation of their behavior. Cultural norms such as self-reliance have sometimes been called ideal values, those which the person strives for but does not expect to achieve. In other instances Americans invoke cultural norms which furnish genuine references to the individual's behavior; the cultural norm coincides with a value in a specific situation. Progress, for instance, freely invoked and emotionally laden, is a valid reference for the behavior of most Americans when it is used to refer to a high valuation of technological and material improvement.

---

*To many, perhaps most Americans, self-reliance connotes an extreme form of independence — the attitude that led the early pioneer to move on when he could smell the smoke from a neighbor's fireplace. Frequently, this is explicit in their definitions of the term.

In cases where a disparity exists between behavior and the values invoked to justify it, we will introduce the term "cultural norm." This term will focus upon what is done, and avoid a search for the assumptions and values that systematically summarize it. "Cultural norms" will be used most often where adaptation of values to specific situations is concerned.

The distinction between cultural norms and cultural assumptions and values deserves emphasis. Americans are aware of their own cultural norms and readily use them to describe their own actions. Members of a culture, however, are not necessarily aware of the assumptions and values which systematically describe their behavior. These are inferences made by the social scientist, about which the individual does not have to be articulate. The only requirement is that the behavior of the individual be describable according to the assumptions and values. As a matter of fact, awareness of the cultural underpinnings of behavior ranges from the very explicit to the implicit. The assumptions in particular are not likely to be acknowledged by members of a culture. Being fundamental to the individual's outlook, they are likely to be considered as a part of the real world and therefore remain unquestioned.

Behavioral Prescriptions

In concluding this discussion of assumptions and values, it is appropriate to raise the possibility of providing the American going abroad, or the foreigner in the United States, with a list of **do's** and **don't's**. Why not tell the American never to point his feet at a person when in Thailand; don't pat a child on the head in Laos; always use polite and flowery expressions in speaking; and do not expect punctuality. In short, it should be possible to draw up a list of behaviors ranging from those that are desirable to those that are taboo. This approach, however, is not commendable for several reasons.

The classification of behavior as desirable or taboo endows it with misleading objectivity. Behavior is ambiguous: the same action may have different meanings in different situations, so that it is necessary to identify the context of behavior and the contingencies of action before the advisor can be armed with prescriptions for specific acts. Fulfillment of this strategy is impossible since the enumeration of possible events lies beyond the state of the knowledge of human behavior. In addition, knowledge of the person with whom the advisor will be working would be required. This information is seldom available and when found is inadequate.

When behavioral prescriptions are discarded, the problem of the overseas advisor is redefined to accentuate diagnosis of problems and prognosis for alternative courses of action. Mere mastery of desirable and taboo actions falls short of equipping the American for effective interaction with his counterparts. It can be argued, in fact, that the overseas advisor—or innovator—should neither act as an American nor as a native. In particular, going native is neither possible nor desirable (Useem **et al**., 1963). The advisor or innovator holds a unique position in which appropriate behavior cannot be derived from lists of desirable and taboo behaviors in the duty country.* More logically, he should

---

*See Kunkel, 1965, for the behavioristic position in the area of innovation.

adopt a third culture based on expanded cross-cultural understanding. The first step in doing this is to understand the assumptions and values on which one's own behavior rests. It is our intention here to aid the reader in the development of that understanding.

Similar conclusions can be reached regarding the foreigner living in the United States and his advisor. There are some clear **do's** and **don't's** in the United States but the pluralism and practicality of American life can be bewildering to the foreigner. The informality of American social relations may be perceived as chaotic and the avoidance of overt authority may be appraised as ambiguity. Americans seen through foreign eyes appear to live without firm guidelines and hence their behavior seems variable and uncertain. The foreign student advisor occupies a difficult position if he attempts to prescribe specific behavior. He, like the American abroad, should strive for cross-cultural understanding, seeking to comprehend the basis of his own behavior and compare it with those other other cultures — and encouraging foreign students to do the same.

Effective behavior in a third-culture situation can only emerge from sound cross-cultural understanding.

Part II
PATTERNS OF THINKING

Cultural differences in patterns of thinking are important issues for both the American advisor working abroad and in the United States with persons from abroad. The issue perhaps arises in clearest form in the educational environment since it is the American instructor or advisor who frequently recognizes that the performance of the foreign student reflects a particular pattern of thinking. Outside the educational situation, the foreigner and the American usually work together under circumstances where political, social or economic factors may be more salient than they are in the instructor or advisor relationship. In these situations, differences in patterns of thinking are frequently perceived as unfavorable personality or social traits. The other person, American or foreigner, may be perceived as irrational, uncultured, arrogant or antagonistic. These descriptions do not exhaust the range of depreciatory reactions elicited by differences in patterns of thinking. Since the educational environment is partly insulated from competitions other than those for knowledge, skills and intellectual analysis, it facilitates the recognition and understanding of cultural differences in thinking.

1. DIFFERENCES IN STYLE

Foreign students are frequently described by American instructors as lacking "analytical thinking." In writing papers, theses and dissertations, the students tend to be subjective and descriptive. They avoid analysis and, when compelled to do so, make inappropriate generalizations. A less frequent complaint — usually made about some European students, is that they are too theoretical, disparage facts, and ignore methods for collecting data. These two observations suggest that the preferred American pattern of thinking—that which is dominant in the academic world and, to a great extent, represents the cultural norm — lies in-between theoretical speculation and empirical description.

Americans are distrustful of theories which seem remote from some kind of application. The role of concepts and ideas in American life is to provide direction for instrumental activity. Ways of thought are judged and tested by their ability to become embodied in institutions and to be put into practice. The role of the American intellectual over the span of American history has been precarious (Cohen, 1954, 37-51). He has been consistently pressed to show the utility of his ideas and theories — unlike the intellectual in many countries of Europe who earns respect for his work distinct from its practicality. Americans usually have discarded the European tradition of evaluating ideas or systems of thought according to "intellectual consistency" or "aesthetic appeal" (Boorstin, 1960, 57).

For Americans, the world is composed of facts — not ideas. Their process of thinking is generally inductive, beginning with facts and then proceeding to ideas. But the movement from the concrete to the more abstract is seldom a complete success, for Americans have recurrent need to reaffirm their theories and, as has been noted, their ideas require validation by application and by becoming institutionalized. The point of origin in thinking is not as concrete as Americans frequently believe. American pragmatism cannot match the unswerving attachment to the concrete facts of life demonstrated by Chinese patterns of thinking. In comparison, American patterns appear theoretical and abstract. It is the operational quality of American thinking that makes it unusual, the incessant need to systematize the perception of the world into a form that enables the individual to act. The perception and thinking of Americans typically assumes a perspective of an observer or agent and it is seldom that the world is appraised and considered in a concrete and objective manner. This operational aspect of American thinking can be demonstrated by examples from behavior to technology.

This American tendency to assume an operational perspective is well brought out in how roads are marked when undergoing repair. The practice followed requires that a sign announcing the repairs be placed at the last point at which the motorist may choose an alternative route. It is not the road repair that is announced, in a sense, but the last choice available to the motorist because of the repairs. In placing the sign, the road crew imagines the motorist driving towards the site of the repair and positions the sign for his benefit. In other parts of the world, and sometimes in the United States as well, the sign is placed so that it accurately indicates the site of the repairs. The sign describes the world and ignores the person who will have to take action in that world — at least, it ignores his ability to make choices.

The operational style of thinking leads to a stress on consequences and results in a disregard for the empirical world as such. What is important is the ability of the individual to affect the empirical world. In contrast to the American operational style of thinking, the European tends to attach primacy and reality to ideas and theories. His deductive and abstract style of thinking gives priority to the conceptual world. Although the empirical world is not necessarily disdained, it is treated with a symbolic and demonstrational attitude. The deductive thinker is likely to have much more confidence in his ideas and theories so that it suffices for him to show one or two connections between his concepts and the empirical world. He does not feel compelled in the American way to amass facts and statistics. He prefers to generalize from one concept to another one, or to facts, by means of logic. He has a faith and trust in the powers of thought which the American places upon his methods of empirical observation and measurement.

There is a tendency for the deductive individual to consider ideas as parts of the world of reality, to consider them as organic and alive. He may consider a new idea to be a "revelation" or a "discovery" while the more inductive American thinker will consider a concept more in the nature of a "construct" or an "invention." It frequently remains vague and ambiguous, defined by examples. This difference in styles of thinking may be illustrated by the comment of an American sociologist on the observation by Ferdinand Tonnies, a European, that "in the organic world the concept itself is a living reality." Martindale, in part, observes that "presumably the concept of a man, like an actual man, gets up in the morning, puts on its pants, shaves, and in other ways prepares for a busy day" (Martindale, 1960, 91).

The American way of thinking produces disciplines in the social sciences that are more likely to be empirical and to stress methods than the same disciplines in European countries. For the European social scientist, empirically-based concepts are easily referred to philosophical issues. Scientific work is often seen as confirming and elaborating the organic theories of other scientists and philosophers.

The discussion of induction and deduction has thus far drawn contrasts between American and European styles of thinking. These crude comparisons are not intended to suggest there is a single style of thinking characteristic of Americans and another of Europeans. At this point it becomes important to indicate variation within American patterns of thinking and in the direction of the foreign students whom American instructors describe as lacking ''analytical thinking.''

In a recent study, children from low-income homes attending school in Pittsburgh, Pennsylvania, were found to have two different conceptual styles which incorporate some of the features of patterns of thinking encountered in different societies. Rosalie Cohen, the investigator, defined conceptual styles as ''integrated rule-sets for the selection and organization of sense data'' (R. Cohen, 1969, 841). Within each conceptual style, certain assumptions and relationships are logically possible and others are not. Furthermore, the styles can be defined ''without reference to specific substantive content and they are not related to native ability'' (R. Cohen, 1969, 841-842).

Cohen's investigation of conceptual styles yields one kind which she called ''analytical,'' corresponding generally to the description which we have given of the dominant American pattern of thinking. In contrast to the ''analytical'' she found a ''relational'' style which is less abstract and more sensitive to total characteristics of things rather than to parts of things (as is the case with the analytical).

Perhaps the most important contribution of Cohen's work is to indicate that these conceptual styles are associated with different family and friendship structures. Persons with relational patterns of thinking came from a background in which neither equality among persons nor differentiation of roles is as accentuated as it is in the background of those with analytical patterns of thinking. Culture groups where the analytical type appears are more formally organized and privileges, responsibilities and status in the groups are distributed in orderly fashion. The individual has a greater freedom to leave his group and to ''refuse to act in any capacity not defined by his job'' (Cohen, 1969, 853). His conceptual style and values are those identified with the American middle class. On the other hand, the relational person is more deeply embedded in his membership groups. He is expected to identify with total group activities rather than with formal functions associated with his role in the group. He must be ready to act in any capacity at any time. Functions in the group, including leadership, are shared more widely among members than is found with groups composed of analytical persons (Cohen, 1969, 844-856).

These distinctions parallel many findings revealed in the study of cross-cultural differences. Ability to show an association between conceptual style and social organization is important in that field. Particularly important is Cohen's conclusion that the schools her children attended and the social institutions which Americans create are particularly suited to the analytical conceptual style. The social organizations, curricula, pedagogy and discipline in the schools provide unfavorable environments for the relational conceptual style. This condition may be very similar to the dilemma of many foreign and American students in higher education. The American instructor who complains that many foreign students cannot think analytically may be referring to the same problem faced by the relational conceptual style found by Cohen among low income children.

The relational conceptual style possesses characteristics similar to those found in accentuated form in the studies of cultural differences. Taking the American middle-class pattern of thinking, characterized by induction, as the point of reference, we can contrast it with the accentuated relational styles of persons from other countries. In his study comparing the East with the West, Northrop asserts that non-Western cultures insist on the immediate apprehension of the world (Northrop, 1946). Intuition or mysticism penetrates to the core of experience and shows it to be one with the observer. Thinking, perception, sensing and experience are part of the same wholeness of existence. Westerners, on the other hand, according to Northrop, introduce a theoretical term which intervenes between the empirical world and acts of observation and thinking. The Westerner is one step removed from experience.

The distinction between inductive and relational styles reveals that one of the differences is the separation of the subjective from the objective in induction. The relational style of thinking rests excessively on experience and fails to separate the experiencing person from objective facts, figures or concepts. The students with relational inclinations — some foreign and some American as well — are said by their instructors to confuse concepts with impressions gained through observation or experience. These students fail to make the distinction between the objective and the subjective which is required in the academic world. In their thinking and writing there is demonstrated an equivalence between experience and empirical facts and both have equal validity with concepts derived from persons in authority.

The Chinese pattern of thinking provides an accentuated example of the relational style, and for this reason, from the Western point of view it lacks clarity. The Chinese do not analyze a topic divisively by breaking it down into parts. Their thinking is based upon concrete conceptions weighted with judgment and lacking the precision and abstraction of Western concepts (Granet, 1950, 8-30). These conceptions lack the power of analysis and classification but, like a proper name in English, excel in identification since they evoke concreteness, emotion and commitment to action. References to the conceptions in the spoken word itself tend to be taken for the act (Granet, 1950, 40). Chinese thought strives for unity between events or objects and their given signs or symbols. An event may be explained by pointing to another event which occurred at the same time, even though by Western logic, the two are not connected. The movement from event to event provides the displacement characteristic of Chinese thought and gives rise to references to it as correlational logic (Tung-sun, 1962, 215). In contrast, Western thought tends to displace along abstract concepts or principles.

It is clear from these brief observations of the Chinese style of thinking that their system of logic will differ from that of the middle-class American. The Chinese are more likely to think by means of analogies and to make greater use of metaphors and similes in drawing conclusions.

2. LANGUAGE: CLARITY AND AMBIGUITY

The color blue gradually merges into green. The difference between the two is continuous since no boundary exists which clearly separates them. When the perceiver reacts as if the two colors can be sharply distinguished, his response is based on an expectation to perceive the environment composed of separate things and concepts. The discontinuity of the environment is the product of categorization and both its development and recognition are facilitated by the use of labels to stand for concepts and things.

Verbal categories and, therefore, language, play a significant role in the recognition of the environment as composed of separate things and concepts. For instance, the use of the names **blue** and **green** facilitates the perception of the difference between the two colors. When perceptions fall between categories used to code visual stimuli — blue-green and green-blue — much information is lost. These ambiguous areas usually receive longer names, observers react slower to them and disagree in identifying them (Brown, 1958, 241).

It is well known that persons and members of various cultures categorize experience in different ways; this is the essential cultural difference. Variations in how the continuum of the environment is distinguished into separate things may contribute to the difficulties of intercultural communication, since the areas of the continuum which are ambiguous are suppressed and become associated with interest and anxiety. In the words of Leach, "Language gives us the names to distinguish the things; taboo inhibits the recognition of those parts of the continuum which separate the things..." (Leach, 1964, 35). Leach provides evidence for this belief from the classification of animals in English.

There are four classes of animals which fall in a series according to their social distance from the human self: pets; tame farm animals; field animals or game; and, remote wild animals. Leach points out that those animals which are ambiguous by classification — that serve to break up the continuity of animals along the dimension of closeness to the self, become recipients of special attention. The dog, for instance, is surely both animal and more than an animal; he is a pet and the companion of man. The dog's affiliation with man places him in the class of "not food" for the English speaker, although in other parts of the world the dog is raised for food. The dog also serves as the source of verbal abuse in phrases such as **son of a bitch**, whereas a clearly remote animal such as the bear does not enjoy similar treatment. Leach writes that:

> In seventeenth century English witchcraft trials it was very commonly asserted that the Devil appeared in the form of a Dog; i.e., God, backwards. In England, we still employ this same metathesis when we refer to a clergyman's collar as a 'dog collar' instead of a 'God collar' (Leach, 1964, 27).

Other animals which share the ambiguity of the dog are the cat, horse, ass, goat, pig, rabbit and fox. Each one of these animals "appear to be specially loaded with taboo values, as indicated by their use in obscenity and abuse or by metaphysical associations or by the intrusion of euphemism" (Leach, 1964, 41).

Another example of the potency of ambiguity is found with the exudations of the human body such as urine, blood, sweat, spittle, nail parings and others. All of these substances occupy an ambiguous position; they are both of the body and yet not of the body. Throughout the world, they are felt to be dirty and also powerful (Leach, 1964, 38). The potential to arouse strong reactions can be tested by the proposal of taking a glass of water, spitting into it and then drinking the water. If the proposed action arouses disgust it should be remembered that drinking the water merely returns the saliva to the mouth. The reaction of disgust is precipitated by the significance of saliva as an exudation of the body.

Thus far, language has been considered as contributing to the process of categorization and, hence, enhancing clarity of perception and thought. Linguistic clarity, however, may derive from habits of language and may represent vagueness or even ambiguity to persons outside the linguistic community. Thus, what Americans consider clear and precise uses of language, appear unclear to Britishers or foreigners who have learned English under British influence. The Americans' use of language tends to be specific to a context and frequently reflects general cultural assumptions and values. The foreigner is puzzled by the vagueness and ambiguity until he has mastered both the context and the culture.

A typical phenomenon among American speakers is the selection of a general noun which lacks precision and to which is added another noun or adjective as modifier. The modifier may be equally vague, but the combination registers precision and "communicates" to the American ear through the phenomenon of "verbal dynamics." The word **students** sounds better as **student body**, and **value**, as **value orientation**. **Science** is often rendered as **scientific method**, and a **book** may become **reading material**. As can be seen from the examples, verbal dynamics include preferred general nouns. Often used are **approach**, **behavior**, **development**, **facilities**, **growth**, **learning**, and **process**. Preferred nouns or adjectives used as modifiers include **dynamic**, **experimental**, **exploratory**, **personal**, **productive**, **operational**, and **self**. Combinations from these two samples of words furnish formidable cultural norms, such as **dynamic process** and **self-learning**. Verbal dynamics often are difficult to translate. The reference in a Washington, D.C. newspaper, to the "traffic-bearing facility" over the Potomac, could overburden a language that values precision. This example, however, draws attention to the reasons for verbal dynamics.

Languages apparently pass through different stages of evolution. An early stage, characterized by inflections, yields to a second stage employing prepositions which, in turn, evolves the use of adjectival nouns as represented by verbal dynamics. The Chinese language has evolved along this course and English seems to be pursuing the same path. Linguistic evolution does not explain, however, why Americans should be further along in their verbal dynamics than other English speakers. The disparity has to be explained according to unique features of the use of language in the United States.

The American people have experienced a strong impetus to discard the ways of the old world and adopt those of the new. The immigrants usually encouraged their children to become Americanized and they eagerly accepted the language and the ways of the new country and turned their back on the language and customs of the old. Until recent times, perhaps the United States has been the only country in which to speak two languages was a mark of low status. The impulse to adopt the language of the country, English, was facilitated by an emphasis on simple vocabulary, the disregard for style, and the use of slang as an expression of affiliation and social conformity. American use of English has generally resisted convergence with literary traditions. Even in the areas of the sciences, the language used has been heavily infiltrated by jargon which accomplishes for the scientist professional services parallel to the social function performed by slang. In either case, vocabulary tends to be limited with the consequence that the uses of language are loose and vague. Where an Englishman may say "bestow a prize," the American says "give a prize." The same words are used by Americans in innumerable instances with modifiers attached when necessary to make the meaning more explicit. The Britisher employs vocabulary precisely.

The combination of two or more words in verbal dynamics conveys a feeling of process which more precise words might not suggest. The juxtaposition of two or more words, modifying each other, captures the American preoccupation with processes. A **bridge** is a structural concept; it is a thing. The verbal dynamics of **traffic-bearing facility** shifts the focus from the structure to the functions of the structure. Structure is a derivative of the interaction between the two components of the words; the word **facility** is general and too vague to denote structure. An examination of verbal dynamics usually reveals a loss of precision; the term is understandable only to those accustomed to it and a shift in emphasis from structure and things to process. This explanation of verbal dynamics foreshadows in the uses of language fundamental characteristics of American culture.

3. DICHOTOMIES AND EXPLANATION

It has often been observed that Americans draw a distinction between the subjective and the objective. They also clearly separate "we" from "they" and "our group" from "their group." This differentiation (which is not confined to the "we" versus "they" dichotomy) reflects the tendency of English-speaking peoples to make twofold judgments; this is particularly applicable to Americans. The language itself provides a precedent for it in its clear differentiation of subject and predicate. When there is a predicate in the language but no subject, then one is assumed. The word "it" often suffices for the missing subject, as in the sentence: "It rained." At the level of gross behavior, events or actions also require a "cause" or an agent who may be held responsible. The idea of a natural "happening" or "occurrence" is not a familiar or acceptable one for Americans, as it is for instance for the Chinese. Americans are not satisfied with statements of fact until they have determined who is responsible — who did it or who caused it to be done. "Where there's smoke, there's fire" means that each effect or event has a causative agent.

One more characteristic that Americans display in making judgments clarifies the American style of evaluation. Quite often Americans make a judgment or justify an action with little reference to external relationships, depending solely on personal preference. An example should make this clear. Mead reports that Americans will answer the question, "What is your favorite color?" while Englishmen asked the same question are usually not willing to name a choice without knowing its purpose, since their favorite color depends on the object (Mead, 1947, 140). Whereas the American is willing to consider colors in relation only to his preference, the Englishman apparently is not willing to dissociate the color from the object. The American's focus on the self allows him to combine things and ideas that to others may seem incongruous.

The propensity to make these kinds of judgments is interrelated with the American tendency to see the world in terms of black or white, and in the American character at any rate, it is related to a predisposition to action. That is in part due to the fact that the dichotomies which Americans set up are unequal: one element is usually valued more than the other. This characteristic can be seen in the following dichotomies: work-play, good-evil, peace-war, military-civilian, right-wrong, successful-unsuccessful, and man-nature. These polarities simplify the view of the world, predispose to action and provide Americans with their typical method of evaluating and judging by means of a comparison. This style of evaluation is so pervasive that it deserves elaboration.

The American advisor overseas is likely to evaluate his counterparts according to the norms of the United States and to decide accordingly that they are better, the same or worse. He is likely to give advice on the same basis: "You should do thus-and-thus because that is the way it is done in my organization" or "in the United States." The implicit American standard is used throughout for making estimates and justifying advice. The American resists describing or judging something in terms of itself or in its own context. Instead, he insists on a comparison. He evaluates himself against others like himself; he judges a movie against other movies he has seen; he judges his children against the norm for their age; and then, most naturally, he judges other people against Americans. The evaluation of "good because" is more naturally rendered as "good as."

The constant mention of American values or of previous experience of the advisor may well aggravate the position of the advisor or consultant, which is a delicate one at best. Regardless of the American's attitude, his very presence suggests that he has knowledge or skills that the local people do not have. The American, by his mere presence, is already precariously near to suggesting implicitly that he is superior to the local people; and when he evaluates and justifies through a comparison with American norms, he implicitly suggests his standards are better. The situation is similar for the foreign student advisor.

It is perhaps this tendency which has partly contributed to the American reputation for moralizing and arrogance. Whenever Americans observe graft, unusual sexual behavior, cruelty, an unfamiliar life-style, or a different way of planting a crop, they tend to make comparisons on the basis of their conception of American behavior in a similar context. They subsequently arrive at a judgment of good or bad which may mean immoral in one instance or "it doesn't work" in another. The American usually does not take into account the fact that what he observes overseas is the behavior of members of another culture. He makes a direct comparison and draws a conclusion from it, whereas a Chinese for example is likely to say "that is American" rather than "that is bad." Completely oriented to the situation, the Chinese might judge the context to be inappropriate but would avoid labeling it bad. The implication would be that at the proper place and time it would be appropriate. In the words of an anthropologist comparing the American and the Chinese:

> ...The usual Chinese description of things American is that they are different; but the usual American view of the Chinese is that they do everything in the wrong way (Hsu, 1953, 92).

In the comparative judgment favored by Americans, things are compared with other similar things. But when an individual possesses some kind of criterion against which he evaluates an issue or thing, he makes an absolute judgment — as illustrated by the following example from Thailand. It occurred with American Peace Corps volunteers who were sent to work alongside Thai instructors teaching English as a second language. A Peace Corps representative from Washington went to Thailand to appraise the effectiveness of his volunteers. When he asked the Thai supervisor about the Thai instructors of English, the answer was likely to be, "Well, Mr. A. is an excellent instructor, and Mr. B. is a good instructor (or a poor instructor)," thereby giving the American representative an absolute judgment. The instructor was judged against a quality of goodness in being a teacher.

The example is important because the Thai supervisor gave a different kind of answer when asked about the American Peace Corps volunteers teaching English alongside the Thai instructors. He observed that: "Mr. Smith is as good as (or worse than) Mr. Jackson." In other words, he switched to the typically American comparative style of making judgments when evaluating Americans.

It is important to stress that the Thai used two kinds of judgments, illustrating the thesis that there is no particular psychological or cultural characteristic adhered to by all members of a given ethnic group. Variation is the very essence of culture and any culture contains all, or nearly all human possibilities.

An evaluation frequently implies giving explanations to sustain the judgment. What kind of information or reserve of meaning is tapped in providing an explanation? As we have seen, the American use of comparative judgments avoids appeals to intrinsic values. The thing evaluated is compared to other similar things with the individual making a choice on the basis of personal preference. Although Americans may not recognize it, they tend to formulate problems, seek solutions and make choices most readily at the economic and technological levels.

Comparative judgments stress present evaluations according to competing interests or groups while disparaging an evaluation in historical depth. This is illustrated by a Turkish student attending an American university. He spoke out in class following a presentation by the instructor on achievement motivation in contemporary American life. The Turkish student agreed but suggested that achievement motivation derived from conditions existing during the Middle Ages. He spoke for about ten minutes, showing a good mastery of his subject. His comments referred to different subjects and ages and did not, in any precise sense, chronologically derive achievement motivation from the Middle Ages.

When he had finished an American student observed, "I agree with you, but why go so far back?" It was clear that the American students in the class did not appreciate the Turk's use of history as a reserve of meaning. Examples, events, personages — referred to without too much attention to chronology — provided him with both rhetoric and meaning for grasping the significance of achievement motivation in American life. In contrast, the American students preferred to view achievement motivation in its contemporary form, or, if they turned to history would derive it chronologically as a chain of cause and effect from the past.

Part III
AMERICAN ASSUMPTIONS
AND VALUES

The components used to analyze a given cultural pattern are arbitrary and depend to a large degree on the purposes at hand. For this report, four different components have been used: **form of activity**, **form of relation to others**, **perception of the world**, and **perception of the self**. The first component, the form of activity, is the link between the individual and the concrete event in the world. It reflects the other assumptions in the context of a specific moment and place and the demands of a given situation.

Each component of a culture affects the others and, in turn, is limited by them. (Variations in the same components also exist within the same pattern.) Contradictions among assumptions and values are probably universal throughout societies. In American culture, for instance, the stress on the value of **equality** among all is sometimes incompatible with **achievement** and, also, **freedom** (Williams 1964, 27-28).

Despite internal variations and contradictions, there is an overall integration to the pattern of middle-class American culture. It is possible to simplify its description by isolating various components and considering them one at a time. This process involves abstracting from behavior assumptions and values that are probably never found in the pure and isolated form in which they are described. Several cultural assumptions and values are usually necessary to explain the same concrete behavior.

Within each of the four following chapters different aspects of the four components are considered, ranging from the most systematic aspects to those cultural norms which serve merely as platitudes or rallying calls for Americans. The cultural norms do not necessarily provide accurate references for behavior.

1. FORM OF ACTIVITY

Orientation to Action

Action in the real world requires a source since for the American, it does not simply occur. An agent or, in the more abstract sense, a cause is required. More often than not the American does not stop with the identification of the agent of action but continues to search for the background reasons which led the agent to decide to act. Furthermore, the agent exists for the purpose of getting things done. The orientation to action, or the phase preceding behavior, is frequently conceived as decision-making or problem-solving. Both of these concepts are vague in meaning and they are employed indiscriminately by Americans to refer to cultural norms of the society. Decision-making includes a loose constellation of both assumptions and values in American culture and, hence, provides a convenient entry into the subject.

In face-to-face situations the locus of both the action and the decision to act lies with the individual. Its foundation is established early in life. From the earliest age, the American child is encouraged to decide for himself — to make up his own mind; he is encouraged to believe he himself is the best judge of what he wants and what he should do. Even in those instances where the American cannot decide for himself, he still prizes the illusion that he is the locus of decision-making. Thus, when he needs to consult a banker, teacher, counselor or expert of any kind, he perceives it as seeking information and advice that helps him to make up his own mind. The expert is treated as a resource person and not as a decision-maker. The American believes, ideally, that he should be his own source of information and opinions and, also, solve his own problems. Esthetic judgments are frequently equated with personal preferences, since the American often resents accepting canons for judging the worth of a work of art. He prefers that value reside in the self; if the individual likes it, it is good. The result is an intense self-centeredness of the individual — so striking that an American psychologist has suggested this as a universal value (Rogers, 1964, 166).

Although American culture provides examples of situations in which another person decides for the individual who is chiefly affected by the decision, more striking instances of this kind of displacement of decision-making usually occur in non-Western countries. In many parts of the world parents choose a wife for their son. In this and in many other situations, the decision-maker is not the person most affected by the decision but the occupant of a traditional role in the social group — in the example above, the parents.

Another variety of decision-making prevalent both in the United States and in the non-Western world is that in which decision-making is localized in a group. More kinds of decisions are likely to be made by the group in a non-Western society than in the United States. Many matters that require action by a family or community in the non-Western world will be settled by a private decision among Americans. Furthermore, the manner in which the individual participates in the group may differ considerably among societies. The American usually expects to be able to express his opinion and to exert a fair influence in the final decision. To fulfill his expectations, an American can be quite concerned with "matters of procedure," with "agenda" and voting procedures. These concerns are not ritualistic or ceremonial as they may be in some cultures, but are for the purpose of ensuring fairness to all and facilitating action. Even when bypassing formal procedures, the American is persuaded by the appeal to give everybody a chance to speak and an equal voice in the decision. When interacting with members of different cultures who do not hold the value of fairness and equality for all members of a group, or who do not discriminate between means and substantive questions, the American may be accused of subterfuge or evasiveness when he raises matters of procedure or agenda. (See Glenn, 1954, 176).

The American value of majority rule is not universal. The Japanese reject the majority voice in decision-making, which becomes binding upon both the majority and minority alike. Rafael Steinberg writes:

> One Western concept that has never really functioned in Japan, although written into constitution and law, is the idea of majority rule. The Confucian ethic, which still governs Japan, demands unanimity,

and in order to respect the "rights of the minority" the majority will compromise on almost every issue until a consensus of some kind is reached.

This principle applies not only to government, but to business board rooms, union halls, association meetings and family councils. No one must ever be completely defeated, because if he is, he cannot "hold up his face."*

In American society the participation of many members of a group in a decision ideally is based on the assumption that all those, insofar as possible, who will be affected by a decision are capable of helping to make it. Overseas, the group's function in decision-making may be quite different from American expectations. A group meeting, ostensibly held to reach a decision, may represent only public confirmation of a decision previously made in privacy by critical members of the group. In addition, the deliberations of the group may be neither substantive nor rational according to American concepts.

In certain areas of American life, decisions are reached by a process significantly different from those described above. The first point of difference is the locus of decision-making: in the examples mentioned the individual took part in the decision as a person, as a vote or as the occupant of a role. The American doctor, however, reaches a decision about his patient's symptoms in a different manner. The patient's report and the doctor's observations are matched against categories of diseases. The doctor's diagnosis and pre-scription follow automatically from the particular category in which the constellation of symptoms fall. When the fit is not close between symptoms and categories defining disease, the doctor may call certain symptoms "benign," a label indicating the lack of correspondence between symptoms and disease categories. The process by which the doctor makes his diagnosis and prescrip-tion is pertinent because it conforms with the manner in which people in the non-Western world habitually reach decisions. The individual merely applies pre-established principles to classify an issue; his actions follow from the result of the classification. Normally, Americans reach decisions on the basis of anticipated consequences for the individual.

These points can be illustrated in the following example taken from an interview with an AID technician in Cambodia charged with training the police:

> When we first tried to get a program of first aid for accident victims going, we did have some trouble because people said if somebody was struck by a car, it was fate, and man had no business in interfering because the victim was being properly punished for past sins. We tried to explain to them that auto accidents are different. They were not due to supernatural intervention, but rather to causes, to viola-tions of the laws. Now we do get policemen to give first aid.

It will be noticed that the technician did not attempt to change the ways of the Cambodians along American lines by emphasizing the personal conse-

---

*In the **Washington Post**, June 7, 1964.

quences of suffering and the danger to the auto victims or by appealing to the personal humanitarianism and sense of duty of the Cambodian policeman. Instead, he modified the scheme of classification by which the Cambodians evaluated an automobile accident and decided that a victim was not their concern. The accident was reclassified into the human sphere, where its effects could be ameliorated by human efforts.

The American locus of decision-making in the individual is paralleled by the insistence that motivation should also arise with him. Responsibility for decision and action devolve on the individual. The idea of individual responsibility is reflected in the typical questions of "Who did this?" and "Who is responsible?" Overseas, where the locus of decision-making is not the individual, the question of responsibility is relatively meaningless. Responsibility is likely to be delocalized in cultures where the people have strong ties to their immediate family or community and reach decisions by consensus.

In Japan, the typical formal or semi-formal group decision is reached by a system that provides for a feeling around — a groping for a voice, preferably the chairman, who will express the group's consensus.

> ...The code calls for the group to reach decisions together — almost by a sort of empathy. The function of a chairman is, therefore, not to help people express themselves freely but to divine the will of the group, to express its will and state the decision reached — presumably on the basis of divined will. This ability of the chairman is called **haragei** (belly art) (Kerlinger, 1951, 38).

The Japanese consider it brash for an individual to make definite decisions regarding himself or others. It is offensive for an individual to urge the acceptance of his opinion as a course of action. He must use circumlocution and maintain a rather strict reserve (Kerlinger, 1951, 38). These features of Japanese decision-making contrast sharply with the American pattern where responsiblity for the decision is normally attached to the individual decision-maker. Among Americans, the individual is ideally the locus both of decision-making and of responsibility for it. The relationship is usually symmetrical although instances occur in which one individual makes a decision while another shoulders responsibility. In Government circles, for instance, it is not unusual for an administrator to call in an individual who is asked to make a decision on a given issue. Once the decision is reached, the decision-maker departs, leaving the issue and decision in the hands of the administrator.

Among the Japanese, the relationship between loci of decision-making and responsibility is asymmetrical. The individual Japanese is subjugated to the group and, when faced with a decision leading to action, he

> ...shrinks and may go to what seem fantastic lengths to avoid making a decision. Even if he should commit himself verbally to a course of action he will frequently end by doing nothing. He lacks a sense of personal responsibility; he feels only a sense of group responsibility. If at all possible, he will try to throw the onus of decision responsibility on a group or, at least, on some other person (Kerlinger, 1951, 37-38).

The Japanese pattern of decision-making is to some degree characteristic of all peoples whose self-reference is the group or for whom decisions should be unanimous — the Samoans, for example (Goodenough, 1963, 511-515).

The American's concept of the world is rational in the sense that he believes the events of the world can be explained and the reasons for particular occurrences can be determined. It follows, then, that certain kinds of training and education can prepare the individual for working in the real world. Experience itself is not the only source of effective performance. Training and education and the kind of knowledge the American values must be practical and applicable. Overseas, the American advisor is prone to act on his rationalism and knowledge, believing that in dealing with non-Westerners it is sufficient to tell them what they should do and how to do it. The assumptions and values of the non-Westerner are often ignored.

The stuff of rationalism turns out to have a typical American flavor, eventually derived from the assumption that the world is mechanistic and the things worthy of effort are material. It is saturated with facts, figures and techniques, since the American's tendency is to be means-oriented toward the world. He is not a philosopher or logician. He is impatient with theory; instead, he conceives of the technological goal of the material world in terms of problems which a rational problem-solver can solve.*

Since it is a popular and pervasive cultural norm, the conceptualization of the world in terms of problems is difficult to evaluate. Perhaps only the foreigner who has failed to exploit its terms can effectively analyze it and then oppose it. His resentment would stem from the realization that his country, himself and his work, all differently, may be problems for his American counterpart. It is this focus that arouses resentment in the counterpart when he recognizes he is a problem — an obstacle in the American's smooth path. This conceptualization of the world in terms ripe for action is likely to give rise to a feeling of depersonalization and a lack of proper regard for others and their ascriptions. The distinguishing aspect of a "problem" is that it includes anything and everything which impinges upon it.

In decision-making the individual focuses on the preliminary step to action whereas conceptualizing the world in terms of "problems" shifts the focus to the action itself.

Usually, the American does not conceive of only one possible course of action for a given problem. Instead, he tends to conceive of alternative courses of action and chooses one. His attitude is comparative; a particular course of action is best for a given purpose rather than the only one. The notion of absolute rightness is repugnant to Americans in the world of action; a purpose for judging the action is present if only implicitly (see Glenn, 1954).

The concept of a plan for action leads us to the idea that action (and, indeed, the world itself) is conceived of as a chain of events. The term "course of action" already suggests this. In the ideal form, the world is seen as a unilateral connection of causes and effects projecting into the future. Since the American focuses on the future rather than on the present or the past, the

---

*A means orientation, like the concept of **problem**, carries a meaning similar to that of the term **operationism**.

isolation of the critical cause becomes paramount. If events in the world are conceived in terms of a multiplicity of causes or even, more radically, in terms of multiple contingencies, as with the Chinese, planning and the control of events and actions become more difficult. The action orientation of the American, therefore, is conducive to a concept of a simple cause for events conceived as a lineal chain of cause and effect.

The final aspect of the American's orientation toward action is his emphasis on choice. After anticipating the future and, specifically, the consequences or effects of his actions, he then chooses that course which will produce the preferred consequences. His conception of desirable consequences is arrived at through a practical empiricism. The effects desired are preferably visible, measurable and materialistic. While the material or empirical effects are more or less objective, what is practical is not. What is practical for one person may not be practical for another. Practicality refers to the adjustment to immediate situations without consideration for long-term effects of theoretical matters. The means-orientation or operationism of the American from the point of view of the non-Westerner often appears to sacrifice the end for the means.

Variations of Form of Activity

The foreign visitor in the United States quickly gains an impression of life lived at a fast pace and of people incessantly active. This image reflects that **doing** is the dominant activity for Americans. The implicit assumption that "getting things done" is worth while is seldom questioned (Kluckhohn and Strodtbeck, 1960, 17).* The ramifications of the **doing** assumption impinge upon other values and assumptions of the culture and pervade the language of Americans, as in the colloquial exchanges of greeting: "How're you doing?" "I'm doing fine — how are you coming along?" All aspects of American life are affected by the predominance of **doing**.

> ...Its most distinctive feature is a demand for the kind of **activity** which results in accomplishments that are measurable by standards conceived to be external to the acting individual. That aspect of self-judgment or judgment of others, which relates to the nature of **activity**, is based mainly upon a measurable accomplishment achieved by acting upon persons, things or situations. What does the individual do? What can he or will he accomplish? These are almost always the primary questions in the American's scale of appraisal of persons (F. Kluckhohn, 1963, 17).

Kluckhohn's definition of **doing** is compatible with other characteristics of Americans such as the importance of achievement, emphasis on visible accomplishments, and the stress on measurement. **Doing**, however, is not to be interpreted as a member of an active-passive dichotomy, since people who are not distinguished by this form of activity can be very active (F. Kluckhohn and

---

*The component of form of activity is a rewording of Kluckhohn's value-orientation — activity. The three variations also come from her as well as the important distinction between **doing** and **action**.

Strodtbeck, 1961, 16). The converse can also hold — some persons who are oriented toward **doing** can be relatively inactive. In American culture, however, along with the assumption of doing, there is a dominant value of "keeping busy." "Idle hands are the devil's workshop." Approximate synonyms to "keeping busy" approach the status of accolades, as when someone is described as "active" or "energetic." Being active may also refer to career-related activity. When a man is characterized as no longer "active" what is frequently meant is that he has retired. Both the assumption of **doing** and the value of being active are dominant patterns in American life.

In the non-Western world, the two remaining forms of activity, **being** and **being in becoming**, are dominant (Kluckhohn and Strodtbeck, 1961, 15-17). Quite often it is the contemplative man, the intellectual, who is prized, rather than the cultural hero of the American — the man who performs visible deeds. Differences in values and assumptions regarding what are the qualities of a leader sometimes confuse Americans overseas who expect the influential persons in a community to be men distinguished by doing. Quite often, however, it turns out to be the intellectual or the man who contemplates and meditates who is respected, honored and listened to.

> In the being form of activity, there is a preference...for the kind of **activity** which is a spontaneous expression of what is conceived to be "given" in the human personality. As compared with either the **being in becoming** or the **doing** orientation, it is a nondevelopmental conception of **activity**. It might even be phrased as a spontaneous expression in **activity** of impulses and desires; yet care must be taken not to make this interpretation a too literal one (Kluckhohn and Strodtbeck, 1961, 16).

Concrete behavior usually reflects several assumptions and values simultaneously. Pure impulse gratification of the **being** form of activity is restrained by the demands of other assumptions and values (Kluckhohn and Strodtbeck, 1961, 16).

The notion of being is very similar to, if not identical with, self-actualization — "the motivational and cognitive life of fully evolved people" (Maslow, 1968, 72). Maslow's description of the experiences of self-actualizing people — or the rare, peak experiences of most people — can be interpreted as the ideal manifestations of the **being** variation of activity. Maslow cites several features of the peak experience which are frequently described as characteristics of non-American cultures. During peak experiences objects tend to be seen as intrinsic wholes, without comparisons; perception can be relatively ego-transcending, appearing unmotivated; the peak experience is intrinsically valued and does not need to be validated by the reaching of goals or the reduction of needs; during the peak experience the person is fused with the experience which occurs outside the usual coordinates of time and space (Maslow, 1968, 74-76). These characteristics of experience are similar to descriptions given by persons who come from societies where **being** is assumed to be the proper form of activity.

A focus on the person is found with the **being in becoming** form of activity. This is in contrast with **doing**, as we have seen, which emphasizes visible and measurable actions. **Being in becoming** introduces the idea of development of the person, which is absent in the other two forms. It emphasizes:

>...that kind of activity which has as its goal the development of all aspects of the self as an integrated whole (Kluckhohn and Strodtbeck, 1961).

All aspects of the personality receive due attention. The intellect, emotions and motives are seen as synthesized into a developing self.

Work and Play

One of the most important distinctions in the forms of activity in American life is the separation of work from play; application of this two-fold judgment yields an unbalanced dichotomy. Work is pursued for a living. It is what a man must do and he is not necessarily supposed to enjoy it. Play, on the other hand, is relief from the drudgery and regularity of work and is enjoyable in its own right although many Americans engage in recreation with the same **seriousness** of purpose expended on work. The American overseas often finds this distinction between work and play absent in the men with whom he associates. His counterpart may appear to take work very casually. Non-Westerners do not usually allow work to interfere with the amenities of living and are, also, likely to expect the foreign advisor to integrate his own personal life and work. In Latin America the American who calls upon a businessman encounters difficulties in expeditiously concluding his agenda. The Latin makes the meeting into a social event and, hence, does not feel compelled to be brief and businesslike in his conversation (Hall and Whyte, 1960). Essentially, the Latin does not make the American discrimination between work and play (or business and play). In each case, the view regarding activity matches the definition of the person provided by Latin and by North American cultures.

Temporal Orientation

The American's concepts of work and action are attached to his orientation toward the future. The unpleasantness which may be connected with work and the stress of doing result in the cultural values of change and progress. These values, however, are not part of societies which look either to the present (as in Latin America) or the past (China, for example) and, hence, tend to focus on immediate conditions or on traditions rather than the intermediate steps required for change and progress toward the future. These differences in temporal orientation are distinguishing marks of cultures and are very important since time is a major component in any constellation of values. For Americans, as an illustration, the orientation toward the future and the high value placed on action yield the principle that one can improve upon the present. Action and hard work will bring about what the individual wants; hence, Americans are described as having the attribute of effort-optimism (C. Kluckhohn and F. Kluckhohn, 1947). Through one's effort or hard work one will achieve one's ambitions. No goal is too remote, no obstacle is too difficult, for the individual who has the will and the determination and who expends the effort. Hard work is rewarded by success. The converse also holds — failure means the individual did not try hard enough, is lazy, or is worthless. These harsh evaluations may be moderated, since one can have bad luck. Nevertheless, they remain as vital American values which shed light on the frustrations of many American advisors in trying to initiate action and attain achievements with a people who are oriented to the past or present, who assume a fatalistic outlook toward the future and whose individualism is upset by the American drive and energy.

Effort-optimism, with its underlying orientation toward the future, gives rise to one of the most frequent and pervasive problems for overseas advisors who often complain about the delays and dilatoriness involved in trying to accomplish anything. The American finds it difficult to adapt to the frustrations that accompany giving advice to people of different cultural backgrounds with the consequence that the morale of the advisor is impaired and his optimism is dampened. His failure to achieve strikes at the heart of his value system. Think, too, of the foreign student advisor who fails to get results. The foreign student may be placing greater importance on his relationship with the advisor or others with whom he is associated than on **doing** what is suggested.

Some advisors interpret their experiences overseas in terms of the long-range effects their work will have. Others point out that their mere presence and personal example were beneficial. A third way of avoiding the consequences of failure is to interpret the mission overseas as a learning situation. The next mission will be more successful, since the advisor has profited from the frustrations and experiences of the last one. This reaction makes use of the American values of training and education as well as the orientation toward the future — in this case, the next mission.

Motivation

Doing describes what a person does to express himself in action of some kind. As we have seen, however, Americans insist on identifying an agent who can take purposeful and sequential action. The concepts of **motive** and **motivation** provide the link between action on the one hand and the agent (and his purposes) on the other. Motives are attributes of the individual which arouse him to action. The concept of motivation reveals the connection and direction in a sequence of actions and, in everyday life, provides a convenient explanation for performance. It is appropriate to say someone succeeds or excels because he is well motivated. The observation is usually a tautology, since the inference about motivation is commonly derived from the performance and not independent knowledge of the individual. As commonly used, however, it is not questioned.

The importance of motivation in American society may well be associated with the phenomenon that the self-images of Americans tend to be general and vague. Motivation helps to fill this void, since it is a dynamic concept that associates the self with action and leads to the belief that the self is what the self does. The fulfillment of the individual, isolated in a mechanistic world, is attained in achievement — the motivation that propels the American and gives the culture its quality of "driveness" (Henry, 1963, 25-26). Restless and uncertain, he has recurrent need to prove himself and thereby attain an identity and success through his achievements. Hence, his accomplishments must be personal, visible and measurable, since the culture does not provide a means of evaluating and knowing the self except through externals of performance and attainment. It is this kind of motive which has been called **achievement**.

The achievement motive has been intensively studied in the United States and other societies. The results of the research reported by David McClelland (McClelland, 1961) portray the individual with high achievement motive as a person who enjoys taking the initiative in making decisions. He prefers to participate in activities that challenge his skills and abilities. He is usually confident of success, but tends to be too optimistic when the conditions for a successful performance are unknown. When he possesses information which permits an objective appraisal of success, he is inclined to use it for a rational assessment of the situation, his abilities and skills, and for guiding his performance. Persons with high achievement, often identified with the business or economic entrepreneur, have been described as risk-takers. This attribute emerges from the research studies as a complex quality, subject to many contingencies. McClelland concludes that those who have high achievement motivation appear to prefer situations involving risk "only when they have some chance of influencing the outcome through their own skills and abilities" (McClelland, 1961, 214). In this conclusion, the focus returns to the individual.

Although achievement is the dominant motive for Americans, ascription exists as a variation. It is marked by an emphasis on **being**; the individual may be defined as the member of a family, for instance, as is sometimes found in New England and the more traditional-oriented parts of the South, or the individual is defined according to his status or profession, as in the military. It is this kind of motivation, rather than achievement, which is shared by many cultures throughout the world as the dominant motivation. Many of the actions of people in non-Western cultures can be understood as directed toward preserving and enhancing their particular position within the social structure, whereas considerations about tangible progress and improvement are secondary in importance, if present at all.

Individuals with an ascriptive motivation are usually enmeshed in reciprocal relations with members of their family, community or trade and profession. These social links are much more binding than in the case of Americans. In Vietnam, for instance, an operator of a printing shop reports supporting his employees to the limits of his ability for six months after he was put out of business by government action. An American would probably not expect the same responsibility from his employer. When an American joins an organization or a business he does so as a free agent and usually preserves the right to move out whenever his purposes are no longer served by being a member. On the other hand, he usually accepts the fortunes of the organization and, if it fails, then it is up to the individual to find another position. The organization is not expected to maintain its employees on the payroll.

The patron system prevalent in much of Latin America also presents an intricate set of social relations between the individual and the patron. The latter may be the godfather of members of his estate and may extend, as a matter of obligation, personal services and considerations which would be foreign to the American overseer. As with the Vietnamese businessman, the obligations incurred are expected to transcend adventitious events of failure, poverty or change of plans.

Ascriptive motivation introduces assumptions about the sources of action and purposes of behavior which differ from the view implied in the achievement motive. The individual is perceived to belong to a social group and to behave according to the obligations, duties and privileges inherent in his social and professional position. To understand and manage behavior, the American must contend with the psychological predisposition of the person, since motivation is a quality of the individual. In ascriptive societies, however, the sources of motivation are more likely to be in the group or society. In the words of a Ghanaian, an employee of the government, "We do not concern ourselves with motivation, as Americans do. We know what our job is and we do it."

American assumptions regarding the dynamics of behavior are so thoroughly dependent on some motivational concept that it is nearly inconceivable that other people in the world find it more natural to refer behavior to role or social order. Yet, in one work enterprise with Dutch medical missionaries in Africa it was necessary to analyze their work and the problems of their hospital from the perspective of their duties, responsibilities and privileges as doctors, nurses, technicians and administrators of the hospital. An analysis of human relations problems based on conflicting motives of hospital personnel and the consequences for the work and management of the hospital was unconvincing to the Dutch personnel. In American language, it did not communicate. American members of the same medical society, operating a hospital in East Pakistan, perceived their hospital problems in terms of conflicting motives of individuals. Issues of human relations within the hospital were readily perceived as conflict among personal, religious, professional, and social motives of the medical personnel. The Americans then naturally accepted a description of human relations according to a loose analysis of motives. The Dutch rejected the same terms of analysis, since motivation in the American sense was not a significant concept in their thinking.

Measurable Achievement

In American culture, achievement is given a material meaning or, at least, a visible and measurable interpretation. This attitude leads to the American emphasis on technology and, secondly, on publicity — rendering visible unrecognized accomplishments. Acting on these assumptions, technicians and advisors in the field define progress in terms of technological change, more often than not reported in statistical data. Social progress too often comes to mean the number of schools erected, while there is no mention of the training of teachers. The concern with visible achievement often leads the American to lose sight of main issues; he may settle for a sensation, a personal triumph over a counterpart or a specific accomplishment which has visibility and, therefore, can be reported as an achievement. One military advisor is described as becoming personally involved in the choice of headgear for a particular unit, which he finally succeeded in changing. This was his achievement and he was described as determined to have it before his tour of duty was over. Another frequent visible achievement in the military is the building of latrines. This cannot be dismissed as lightly as the incident of the new caps. The persistence of Americans all over the world, however, in building latrines for people who refuse to use them suggests that their appeal as projects may reside in part in their concrete visibility rather than in their potential role in controlling disease.

Since achievement has to be visible and measurable Americans become very sensitive to praise or blame — more so than perhaps any other people except the Japanese. They do not develop the Englishman's self-assurance and the confidence in his own judgment nor the self-sufficiency of the French. They depend on feedback from associates and, particularly, on the visibility of their achievements. Both of these factors are missing in the overseas situation: achievements are usually few and the reactions of one's associates are likely to be both delayed and diffuse (the same is true in many situations for a foreign student advisor). The American advisor is quite often uncertain about the effects, if any, of his advising. His work is incompatible with an achievement orientation, since he should only be a catalyst to his counterpart with the primary function of providing information, skills and judgment rather than concrete achievements. The counterpart is likely to have an ascriptive orientation and, hence, to be somewhat unconcerned with achievements. Deprived of his own visible success and, frequently, not seeing it in his counterpart, the advisor considers himself a failure; Americans find this kind of situation very difficult to handle. They tend to shift their sights to another future achievement or disregard the present situation as the fault of another person. Finally, Americans may face failure with the "let's get the hell out of here" attitude (see C. Kluckhohn, 1954, 120) which may be interpreted as a disguised admission that their actions have been on the wrong track. This suggests one way of removing the stain of failure — that is, by considering it as part of the learning process.

Competition and Affiliation

Competition is the primary method among Americans of motivating members of a group and some have seen it as a basic emphasis in American culture (Potter, 1954, 59-60). Americans, with their individualism and ideas on achieving, respond well to this technique but, where the same approach is applied to members of another culture who do not hold the same values, the effort is ineffective at best and may produce undesirable consequences. People for whom saving face is important or for whom dependency on others is desirable will not accept competition among members of the group with the same enthusiasm as Americans. Thus, attempts to instill a competitive spirit in social, economic or military activities in many non-Western countries, such as Laos and Vietnam, have not been very successful, as the American advisors should have been able to foresee from observing the intense attachment of the people to their family and village. The communal feeling toward each other excludes the incentive to excel over others either as a member of a group or individually. An advisor shows his bewilderment at the Lao's lack of competition in the following words:

> Watching them play a game — volleyball. To us, it's a game. I know when our teams compete, whether it's baseball or basketball — anything, we'd be serious, playing it because we like to win. With

them, they wouldn't be; they would team up and have teams going, but they just didn't give a hoot whether they won or not.

The non-Westerner, with an aversion to competition, is likely to show more strongly developed **affiliation**,* as we have seen, for his own family and community. He knows, and knows of, fewer people than the typical American. Both his direct interaction with others through travel, work and social life and his indirect contact through the mass media are likely to be much more circumscribed than for an American. He will be less self-conscious (see Bell, 1965, 209-212) and less analytical of himself as an individual than the American. Beyond the confines of his immediate world and interest, lies a world largely unknown to him. It is often endowed with danger to the unwary who travels beyond the limits of his own territory. An American advisor in Laos, training the Meo tribesmen for military service, points out that they were effective soldiers only within their own environment. Their knowledge of the outside world was meager and overriden with superstitions which made the soldiers fearful and ineffective in operations outside their own geographical area. Within their own domain, however, their willing acceptance of military discipline and complete dedication to training made them excellent trainees.

The example of the Meo tribesmen is perhaps extreme, but the lack of feeling for being a member of a political entity, a nation, is generally prevalent. This fact is often obscured by the reports in the mass media of instances of intense nationalism on the part of individuals and groups in the non-West. These certainly exist but are not typical of the great majority of the people throughout the world. It is misleading to consider peoples such as the Lao and the Vietnamese to be self-conscious members of their respective countries in the sense that most Americans consider themselves to be citizens of the United States.

Although Americans have been described as primarily motivated by achievement, it does not mean that they do not show some affiliative tendencies. These tendencies, however, are diluted in contrast to the strong social and territorial adhesion found in affiliations in the non-Western world. Margaret Mead describes the American's nostalgia for his home town as symbolic of the question: "Are you the same kind of person I am? Good — how about a coke?" (Mead, 1965, 29). But the preoccupation with the home town is not an establishment of the influence of family and community with defined status and prescribed norms of behavior, as in ascriptive societies. It is instead a way of establishing an affiliation among people who have little in the way of "common origins and common expectations" (Mead, 1965, 30).

It has been mentioned that the values of American culture are changing, that Americans are becoming more group-oriented and less autonomous in their behavior. It is well to point out that in the case of the American military we find a well documented thesis that the primary motivational force for the American soldier during World War II was affiliation. It was not achievement, since military service usually represented an interruption in the typical

---

*Affiliation refers to the social need for the company of others, for companionship; whereas ascription refers to the qualities of being a person, a member of a family, a profession, etc.

American's career and life. Nor was it ascription, since the military usually did not provide a needed or desired identity to be preserved and nurtured. The force to fight for the typical American soldier was derived from a sense of loyalty to the other men in the immediate group (Stouffer **et al.**, 1949). The spread of loyalty was primarily horizontal and based on equality rather than vertical and based on authority. There can be no doubt that affiliation is a motive in other areas of American life and it may be ascendant as American individualism becomes subservient to organization and the goals of groups and institutions.

The Limits of Achievement: The Individual

Externalized achievement is the dominant motivation for the typical American. The pursuit thereof has produced in the United States an unparalleled economic abundance (Potter, 1954, 78-90). It has been argued that the achievement motive provides a key psychological factor in economic development (McClelland, 1961; 61, 105, 157). But hand-in-hand with this motivation there has been in the United States a willingness to exploit and control the physical environment (Potter, 1954, 164-165). These two characteristics of Americans, found as both individual and collective qualities, have been key factors in producing economic abundance.

During their history, Americans have exploited their physical environment as if it were unlimited. The vastness of the land and the opulence of its resources no doubt strengthened the pre-existing belief that the limits to achievement are measured within the individual. The limitations on success are not ascribed to resources, to the actions of others, to the agency of government, nor to fate. For, as the Protestant ethic prescribed, if one has the desire and works hard enough, his labors will be rewarded with success. "Where there's a will, there's a way."

Furthermore, the achievements of the individual are not gained at the expense of others since there enough rewards — material wealth, prestige, popularity — for everyone who aspires and tries. Doctrines such as Marxism which promulgate inevitable conflict among classes because the limited goods of the world are acquired by a few who exploit the masses, have rarely achieved great favor among Americans. Traditionally, Americans have seen failure as a lack of will and of effort on the part of the individual. Successful accumulation of worldly wealth was a sign that the individual belonged to the select group who enjoyed the grace of God. The same idea is still present in a newer version: a rich man cannot be completely bad — or else he would not be rich.

This expansive view of achievement and of a world of economic abundance contrasts sharply with the perception of limited wealth prevalent throughout much of the rest of the world. This latter outlook is more than just a view appropriate to an economy of scarcity in which the individual's aspirations and potential achievements are necessarily limited. It is central to an ascriptive view of society which tends to maintain the status quo in relationships among people. To explain the norms of behavior of such societies, especially those which are traditional and peasant, we turn to George Foster's idea of the Image of the Limited Good. The individual or family that acquires more than its share of a "good," and particularly an economic "good," is viewed with suspicion

(Foster, 1965, 302). Likewise, the individual who accepts a role of leadership will find his motives suspected and

> ...he will be subject to the criticism of his neighbors. By seeking or even accepting an authority position, the ideal man ceases to be ideal. A 'good' man therefore usually shuns community responsibilities (other than of a ritual nature); by so doing he protects his reputation (Foster, 1965, 303).

People do not compete for authority by seeking leadership roles, nor do they compete in material symbols such as dress, housing or food which might make the individual stand out from the rest of the members of the village. The people in peasant villages show a strong desire to look and act like everyone else. By means of uniformity they attempt to be inconspicuous in position and behavior (Foster, 1965, 303).

Despite the stress on conformity in traditional peasant villages, there is a place for individuality. Once a person fulfills the obligation of family, community, and tradition, he may be allowed considerable freedom to express his own individuality. Both conformity and individuality can be found in non-Western societies where the individual is perceived in terms of ascriptive qualities. It is necessary, however, to ascertain for each society those areas in which individuality or uniformity holds.

The motive of achievement, along with its stress on effort, work and the taking of rational risks, is not widely evident outside the West. The individual works to survive, but not to amass wealth, which, like land, is perceived as inherent in nature (see Foster, 1965, 298).

> ... It can be divided up and passed around in various ways, but, within the framework of the villagers' traditional world, it does not grow. Time and tradition have determined the shares each family and individual hold; these shares are not static, since obviously they do shift. But the reason for the relative position of each villager is known at any given time, and any significant change calls for explanation (Foster, 1965, 298).

It follows from the above discussion that innovation or new techniques of working are also not perceived as related to wealth or, in our terms, to achievement. Instead, achievement is a matter of fate, an intervention by an outside agent that does not disrupt the relationships among the members of a community. One such agent is the lottery. By winning, the individual can improve his position without endangering the community (see Foster, 1965, 308-309).

People who have a "lottery" motivation, or a belief in an outside and adventitious intervention in their behalf, are difficult to convince of the virtues of hard work, effort, frugality, and initiative. Even if this attitude does not exist, or if it has been penetrated, the individual may still not accept the necessity of improving his position, for it will extend his obligations. Thus a young Peruvian fisherman refused aid to modernize his fishing technique for the reason that if he had more money he would have more relatives to take care of. He doubted that he would be better off because of his increased responsibilities (Foster, 1962, 92).

An absence of achievement motivation is not necessarily connected to the social and economic conditions of the peasant society. Apparently, a belief in "fate" or "luck" can be found in parts of the non-Western world where density of population and limited land holdings are not a problem. In the interior of Brazil there exists a frontier environment. Land holdings are not limited, population is not dense, and to the west there is new land offering economic opportunities. Yet the people still subscribe to the "luck" motivation, being more concerned with buying tickets for the local game of "bicho" than with developing their local resources or moving west.* It might be argued that the psychological horizon is limited and that they do not recognize that land and economic opportunities are available. Nevertheless, in the same area there is the precedent for squatters' rights. Individuals and families take possession of land, work it, and eventually acquire a right to it. This tradition does not indicate that the possession of land is seen as traditionally limited; there are ways of acquiring it even if the individual is not aware of new land to the west.** This particular case of Brazil suggests that the absence of achievement motivation is not necessarily associated with closed communities of dense population and limited land holdings. Indifference to personal achievement, associated with a belief in "luck," can also be found among people for whom the attitude has little relation to the economic conditions in which they live. It reflects their perception of the self and of the world as well as their concepts of motivation and of fate.

The Limits of Ascription: Total Power

In a society in which motivation rests on an ascriptive base rather than on achievement, cultural norms will be different. Status and inequality will characterize the value system. Each person will have his own fixed position in a vertical, hierarchical tier. In some cases, though not all, as we have seen, ascriptive motivation is associated with an image of a world of restricted resources — in contrast to the American perception of a world of abundance. Some of the permissiveness and competitiveness of American society can no doubt be traced to the belief that there are enough material goods for everyone. David Potter argues that the majority of the world, even Europe, assumes an economy of scarcity, so that the volume of wealth is assumed to be fixed (Potter, 1954, 118). If there is not enough for everyone, if a generous volume of the goods of the society are restricted to only the select few, it is unlikely that the society will countenance perpetual (and probably internecine) competition for the economic and social spoils. It is more sound to assign arbitrarily to each person a status which is transmitted by heredity and rigidly maintained by authority, with both the favored few and the unfavored bulk of the people

---

*Foster, 1965, pp. 308-310, argues that the "brakes on change are less psychological than social" (310). Foster might disagree with the example above. On the other hand, the case of Brazil might be considered outside the scope of peasant societies. Foster stresses limited land holdings and density of population.

**Communication from Charles T. Stewart, Jr.

maintained in their respective statuses from generation to generation.

> ...the status-bound individual often gained a sense of contentment
> with his lot and even of dignity within his narrow sphere, and all that
> he sacrificed for his new psychological advantage was a statistically
> negligible chance for advancement (Potter, 1954, 115).

Within its limits the ascriptive way of life, flourishing in an economy of
scarcity, will most often develop a relatively rigid culture pattern with authority
providing a primary focus. Authority rather than the self or the individual will
become a center for motivation. In contrast, authority in American culture is
seen as a social rather than as a motivational question, since the dominant
pattern in American culture limits the role of authority to providing services,
protecting the rights of the individual, inducing cooperation, and adjudicating
differences. Although many variations on the dominant value exist in American
society — the military for example — or in individuals who prefer strong, clear
authority, these deviant patterns provide little help in understanding the
complete display of authority traditionally found in governments in many of the
countries of Asia, the Middle East and elsewhere. In these states total power
may be vested in the members of the government. The centralized organization
of political and social power permeates the society, profoundly affecting the
way of life of individuals. Considerations of status, loyalty and ascription
replace the American stress on individual competition and achievement.

Delineating a few of the characteristics of a society organized according to
what Karl Wittfogel calls "total power" should be helpful in putting into
perspective American attitudes towards authority as they are contrasted with
those of many non-Westerners. Rather than pick a country which has these
characteristics and contrast it with American patterns, we shall follow Wittfogel's analysis of total power in its political, social, and psychological
characterisics. Wittfogel draws his materials from historical and contemporary
examples and develops a theme regarding total power which, while not fitting
any one society precisely, characterizes in a general way many societies around
the world.

In societies with more or less absolutist governments, political power is
not checked by non-governmental forces found in most Western countries.
Historically the power of the central governments in the West has been limited
by constitutions, large individual landholdings, and political, cultural and
organizational subdivisions. In absolute governments, these checks are generally not present or not effective. Religious and military power are normally
both identified with the state and do not place a check on the government
(Wittfogel, 1957, 49-100). There is no non-governmental center of power
(Wittfogel, 1957, 101-103). Intragovernmental balances such as those found in
the American system also do not exist (Wittfogel, 1957, 101-103). Therefore,
"there develops what may be called a **cumulative tendency of unchecked
power**" (Wittfogel, 1957, 106). The exercise of unchecked authority easily
becomes arbitrary and results in intimidation, secrecy, unpredictability — and
in the extreme, terror and brutality (Wittfogel, 1957, 137, 141). The psychological climate thus created engenders mutual mistrust and suspicion among
officials of the government. The key factor for the official is his relation to the

authority figures (Wittfogel, 1957, 345). Promotions may relate to aptitude but more often depend on the loyalty and subservience of the individual. The prized quality for promotion is "total and ingenious servility" (Wittfogel, 1957, 364).

Parts of the society may lie outside the power system of the absolute state. To varying degrees families and villages, for example, may enjoy autonomy to run their own affairs. There are official requests, impositions from the central government, constables, and often a tax collector, but beyond this outside control usually ends (Wittfogel, 1957, 122-124). The central government does not intrude into those areas where its authority and revenue are not jeopardized.

The people usually have little love for the government and its representatives. The society is clearly demarcated into the ruled versus the rulers, with the people demonstrating a fear of involvement with the government (Wittfogel, 1957, 156). The aloofness of the people from the government and from others with whom specific social relations are not established, may approach pathological proportions from the point of view of the American. Thus assistance to the victim of an accident or a drowning may be withheld for fear that the rescuer will be saddled with the responsibility for the occurrence. The reason for this fear of involvement is certainly not entirely traceable to the nature of authority and of the government, but these are contributing factors. This very brief and simplified description of a state of "total power" is not intended to describe any particular country at any particular point in time. It nevertheless shows us some of the characteristics of states with highly centralized governmental structures and helps us understand certain aspects of the value systems which develop therein. In such countries motivation is rooted in efforts to maintain status and in the personalized ways in which both official and social relations are conducted. There is little incentive for achievement or change. Significant relations are vertical, hence the impetus for successful action, or for change, usually comes from above. There is little precedent for initiative, information, or opinion to originate spontaneously with the people and move upward to the leaders. There are no serious competing interests to the government officials who see the people tied to them by obligations. They do not assume responsibility towards the people in the manner characteristic in more decentralized governments. Government traditionally, as in Burma, for instance, is not concerned with problem-solving or with improving society, but in maintaining loyalty and status (Pye, 1962, 78). Thus authority becomes a source of both social control and motivation.

It is clear from the above examples that the nature of motivation may be quite different in the non-Western countries with centralized governments from what it usually is in the United States. Especially significant is the fact that the definite acceptance of a personal bond between subordinate and superior makes the authority figure an acceptable source of motivation. Direct orders, explicit instructions, and demands for personal conformity may be much more acceptable, and even desired, in the non-Western world than in the United States. American preference for persuasion may be seen as weakness, and self-determination may become egotism and a threat to others.

2. FORM OF SOCIAL RELATIONS

Characteristics of Personal Relations

Personal relationships among Americans are numerous and are marked by friendliness and informality; however, Americans rarely form deep and lasting friendships. Friends and membership groups change easily as the American shifts status or locale; consequently, his social life lacks both permanence and depth (C. Kluckhohn, 1954, 96). Although social activities occupy much of his time, he avoids personal commitments to others. He does not like to get involved. A social act such as an invitation or offered gift is accepted and thanks are expressed. The recipient is not under obligation to reciprocate, although there is present the vague propriety of a return gesture. This social pressure, however, does not have the binding and formal quality of social obligations evident in other cultures. Americans usually prefer to pursue their social life under conditions that minimize incurring social obligations. Gifts, for instance, are customarily given to commemorate a birthday, an anniversary, or a festival such as Christmas. Outside of these well established occasions, circumspection is observed so that giving a gift appears personally anonymous and its significance is carefully limited to avoid a personal meaning that might · be construed as a bribe, seeking special favors, or as requiring reciprocity. In the activity of work, anonymity is commonly achieved by collecting donations from interested people, then awarding the gift to commemorate a specific departure, anniversary or retirement.

The circumspection with which social relations are handled in the United States, so as to avoid obligations, is in direct contrast with conventions in most parts of the world. The American "Thank you; I had a fine time," is insufficient recompense for an evening's invitation. The guest may be expected to bring flowers, as in Germany. And for the non-Westerner, the American's vague feeling that a return gesture is appropriate may be replaced by an importunate obligation. One solution to social obligations, the Dutch treat, may seem crass to non-Americans who prefer the convention of individuals taking turns in being the host in what might be called sequential reciprocity.

In other cultures, the American convention of anonymity in giving gifts is often seen to deprecate the meaning of the act. If the gift does not inconvenience or deprive the donor it has less meaning for the recipient. In parts of India the éxpression for "thanks" does not exist, and social conventions have not required its invention. A social act is seen as the fulfillment of an obligation or a duty which requires no verbal acknowledgement. If the action, as in offering a gift, is not the consequence of an obligation, thanks would still be inappropriate. To imply termination of social interchange by an overt expression of thanks, places a finite value on the gift and cheapens its meaning.

Obviously, social relations among Americans have many variations. The statements made above must be considered as merely suggestive of the dominant pattern in American life, stressing equality, informality, impermanence, and personal detachment in social interaction. One major variant pattern deserves mention. Among the American military, patterns of social relations are in many ways less anonymous and neutral than among typical middle-class Americans. As an officer serves tours of duty throughout the world, he periodically encounters fellow officers with whom he has served before. Quite often strong friendships develop, usually including the entire family. Furthermore, there is a tendency in these relationships to specify expectations of social reciprocities which ordinarily are only vaguely felt by most other Americans. Although one social action does not necessarily require an explicit return gesture, there is the expectation that the association will be actively maintained. These informal social norms may be considered to represent an influence of the explicit and obligatory social conventions of the formal military establishment.

Equality

Running throughout the American's social relationships with others is the theme of equality. Each person is ascribed an irreducible value because of his humanness. "We're all human, after all." Interpersonal relations are typically horizontal, conducted between presumed equals. When a personal confrontation is required between two persons of different hierarchical levels, there is an implicit tendency to establish an atmosphere of equality. Thus even within the definitive authoritarian structure of the military, a commanding officer may ask a subordinate a personal question, or offer a cup of coffee, before beginning a conversation. Furthermore, the officer is not expected to call attention to his rank and authority or exercise his personal power over a subordinate. One mark of a good officer from the enlisted man's point of view is that he does not "pull rank" or "use his authority as a crutch." In short, the good officer promotes a feeling of equality, the preferred social mode among Americans.

Discussing equality in the context of Americans working abroad, Mead says that:

> ...Americans...find it very confusing to shift from high to low status as the situation demands and...respond by a continuous endeavor to stabilize relationships. Their uneasiness often leads to an assertive attempt either to establish a superficially egalitarian ethos — as in the ritual use of first names for everyone, which is most disorienting to persons of many other cultures — or else to an attempt to establish hierarchies which are rigidly resistant to other considerations such as lineage and education (Mead, 1963, 7-8).

It is clear that his cultural values predispose the American to function most effectively on an interpersonal level of equality. He is often confused when confronted with persons of a different status — particularly when that status has been achieved through a legacy of special privileges. The ideal of equality makes it difficult for the American to understand hierarchical patterns of organization overseas, with the consequence that he tends to ignore political questions. He usually does not consider the fact that the loyalty of members of an organization may be the primary principle that explains otherwise unintelligible actions and promotions. Noting the absence of an emphasis on both achievement and equality, Americans may often fail to recognize the characteristics which determine who are the opinion- and decision-makers.

...For instance, that impoverished aristocrats or ascetic priests, beggarly in dress and looks, can still command respect and allegiance, despite their lack of outward signs of visible achievement and "success," is a difficult concept for Americans to grasp. Some people, like the Japanese, present another enigma; for they practice a kind of faceless leadership in which string-pullers exert their authority behind conspicuous but powerless puppet or ceremonial figures in public office (Arensberg and Niehoff, 1964, 135).

The cultural value of equality is restricted in application; it has not extended to some racial and ethnic groups, particularly the Negro. There are also strong hierarchical and authoritarian emphases in large-scale economic and political organizations (Williams, 1961, 441). Beyond these exceptions there remain further reservations to the value of equality. Although all persons are presumed to have equal rights and obligations (Williams, 1961, 442), not everyone is presumed to be of equal talent and ability. The acceptance of inequality of potentialities is tempered by the typical American belief that in any grouping there are people of ability and leadership potential. Their emergence awaits the right opportunity. It is the equality of opportunity that receives emphasis in American culture. Equality does not extend to achievements, success or reward (see Williams, 1961, 442). As we have seen, Americans are usually individually interested in achievement and expect rewards commensurate with their accomplishments.

Although Americans have modified their understanding of equality during their history and have blatantly violated it as well, the value remains a pervasive cultural norm. When working with persons either abroad or in the United States who do not share this value, Americans find it extremely difficult to understand why someone else may comprehend the meaning of equality and still reject it. Persons espousing social hierarchies are likely to believe that equality in social relations is detrimental to structured interactions among persons and hence reduces the predictability of how someone else will act. When social equality prevails, there is a tendency for everyone to be treated alike with little differentiation for personal and social characteristics. Many foreigners resent the sameness of perception and of reaction of Americans, preferring a society which acknowledges social differences among persons.

In the view of sociologist Max Scheler, equality offers a moral value only for that which everyone can do, even the least gifted. If all human beings are equal in moral values and talents then the moral level of the least gifted is the criterion for the worth of all (see Scheler, 1961, 139-144). Scheler finds this view objectionable and argues for what he calls "sacredness," for vitality and spirituality in cultural values (Scheler, 1951, 152). He scorns American commitment to such principles as "utility" as a subordination of ends to means. The views of Scheler lend themselves to a belief in absolute values more agreeable to aristocratic or privileged classes. It is apparent that the thinking of Scheler is abrasive and dangerous for the American system of values. He has been called a "fascist" since his thinking can subsume ideas of cultural and racial superiority. Even though Americans have frequently violated the assumptions of equality, their continued insistence upon it demonstrates their inclination to perpetuate a value in a cultural norm which is part illusion and part reality. Each new generation must grapple with its ambiguity and redefine it for its own purposes.

Confrontation

The indirection of the Japanese, and of all peoples for whom "saving face" is important, contrasts with American assumptions and values ranged around the idea of confrontation — the man-to-man and face-to-face event.

Confrontation in its most direct form begins when someone penetrates the spatial envelope of privacy surrounding each American. When someone draws nearer than about arm's length, the American is likely to interpret this as a sign that he must fight or flee. For this reason the close proximity Latins or Arabs prefer while conversing disturbs Americans, since physical nearness carries either sexual or belligerent meaning.* If the American backs away, then the Latin or Arab may feel that he is being treated with aloofness, if not hostility. In some cultures, however — Thai, Japanese — it is the American who often stands too close during a conversation.

The idea of confrontation goes beyond physical displacement. When faced with a problem, Americans like to get to its source. This means facing the facts, meeting the problem head on, putting the cards on the table and getting information "straight from the horse's mouth." It is also desirable to face people directly, to confront them intentionally.

A contrast to the American values of confrontation is supplied by the indirection of the Japanese in social matters which has been recognized as a technique for accomplishing one's end (Hulse, 1962, 303). Frederick Hulse asserts: "Since so much of overt Japanese culture is purely arbitrary convention which must be accepted like the rule of passing to the right in driving, the importance of objective truth, which must be believed, is relatively minor" (Hulse, 1962, 304). Among the Japanese there even exist rules for what can and cannot be observed. "Guests do not observe their hosts until the latter are properly garbed, as many travelers in Japan have long pointed out" (Hulse, 1962, 304-5). In the highly ritualized culture of Japan, indirection becomes the "conventional method of circumventing convention" (Hulse, 1962, 303). Skill in social maneuvers is esteemed while awkwardness embarrasses friends and is ridiculed by others. A course of action, once embarked upon, should be carried to its logical or extreme conclusion "even if this involves ruthlessness to one's self as well as to others."

> A certain touch of arrogance, a flaunting of one's strength, even a flying in the face of ordinary convention and ritual, can succeed wonderfully simply because it demonstrates one's confidence in his own superior position and ability (Hulse, 1962, 302).

The Japanese concept of "face" has been described as concerned with the status of the self, while the Chinese "face" includes much more concern about the feelings of the other person (La Barre, 1962, 335). La Barre attributes a degree of aggressiveness to the Japanese which has been questioned by other students (see Kerlinger, 1962, 407). The question of "face," however, does represent a phenomenon resulting in indirection in social relations difficult for the American to fathom. Another contrast to the American idea of confrontation is found in many societies such as Thailand in the use of a third party. Business may be conducted with another person by means of an emissary and not directly in a face-to-face confrontation of the principals involved. This indirection extends to aspects of life that the American considers personal and intimate, such as choosing a mate. The use of an intermediary allows both sides mutually to accommodate each other or to withdraw without losing face.

It is apparent that the value of confrontation (versus indirection) has wide ramifications for Americans both overseas and in a home setting with foreign students. It has been noticed even in the use of interpreters. The American sees the interpreter as a window pane that transmits the message from one language to the other; but in cultures where a third-person role is customary, the interpreter's role may become a much more active one, to the consternation of the American who is likely to interpret it as inefficiency or perhaps disloyalty.

Informality and Formality

Another aspect of confrontation is found in the informality and directness with which Americans tend to treat other people. Foreign students in the U.S. frequently have difficulty with this quality until they get used to it. It also has disadvantages in working overseas, for when Americans employ their direct, brusque manners in dealing with other peoples, they are likely to insult or confuse them. The flowery language, complex methods of address, and ritualistic manners found in other cultures reflect the social structure of the people. When Americans fail to use the accepted forms of address, language and manner, they also fail to accord the proper deference, and perhaps worst of all, they violate the prescribed methods of structuring social interactions. Whereas the average American considers formality, style, and protocol as pompous or arrogant, these provide dependable expectations in other cultures of behavior of other persons in social situations.* This function is particularly striking with the Japanese, who cannot communicate until they know the status of the other person since the language requires different forms to correspond to the status of the listener.

The foreigner encrusted by his formality can point to one of the consequences of American informality. Essentially, the American refers to everyone else in the same way; his preferred mode is equality. He reaches a first-name basis readily and early in a relationship. If the American develops a stronger attachment to another person, he may experience difficulty in expressing it. His only channel of communicating to others is direct, unadorned informality. The consequence is that the informality which at first may appear to be a friendly, personal way of treating others contributes to depersonalization, since

---

*Formality tends to be maximal when social interactions are important; few and weak positive ties exist between the participants when the interaction involves relatively severe conflicts of interest or values. (James W. Woodard, "The Role of Fictions in Cultural Organization," **Transactions of the New York Academy of Sciences**, Series II, Vol. VI, No. 8, June, 1944, as discussed in Robin M. Williams, Jr., **American Society**, New York, 1961).

informality — the breeziness, humor and kidding — is extended to everyone alike. Few discriminations are made among people; each one is kept at a depersonalized distance. Even "enemies" are likely to be treated with a controlled friendliness since Americans are usually reluctant to disrupt a social gathering "to make a scene" or "to create a disturbance" by the open show of hostility.

Friendship

The generalized "friend" of Americans, standing for anyone from a passing acquaintance to a life-time intimate, is maintained according to activities. The company of a friend centers around activity, a thing, an event or a shared history. Thus, Americans have friendships which originate "around work, children, or political opinions — around charities, games, various occasions for sharing food and alcohol, etc." (Glenn, 1966, 270). The various compartments of friendship are kept separate, so that a friendship that is centered around the office does not intrude into the relations with friends who participate in recreational activities. Friendship tends to be generalized only to similar activities or events and to persons who have both social and personal commitments to each other. But these patterns of friendships among Americans — particularly the specialization of friends — do not imply a distrust of people. They signify more often the American reluctance to becoming deeply involved with other persons. In circumstances where a foreigner might turn to a friend for help, support or solace, the American will tend to search for the professional, preferring not to inconvenience his friends.

In contrast to the American, the Russian expects to form a deep bond with another person and assumes the "obligation of almost constant companionship, and the rejection of any reticence or secretiveness among friends" (Glenn, 1966, 270). Whereas the American tends to limit friendship to an area of common interest, "The Russian tends to embrace the whole person" (Glenn, 1966, 271). Combining features of both the American and Russian, the French styles of friendship are specialized

> but they also tend to be organized in patterns of long duration, often with an expectation of family friendships extending over more than one generation. Where Americans are competitive even within the group of friends, for Frenchmen as for Russians, friendship excludes competitiveness; the coexistence of cooperation with competition, so natural to Americans, appears incomprehensible to French and Russian informants (Glenn, 1966, 271).

The American and Russian styles of friendship represent consistent patterns, but the French poses contradictions stemming from the simultaneous demands for privacy, independence and long, close friendships. The divergent obligations are reconciled through the French cultural norm of the **brouille**:

> ...friendship is put in abeyance but not broken, the individuals concerned are not on speaking terms, but expect a reconciliation and stand ready to resume mutual help under some grave circumstances

such as death in the family. Under similar circumstances, Americans would quietly drift apart, and Russians seek immediate resolution through a stormy scene (Glenn, 1966, 271).

The nature of the relationship between two people is more precisely defined in many societies outside the West than it is among Americans. Friends may be limited to specific classes of persons instead of to activities. Most frequently excluded are members of the opposite sex. Arab men, for instance, will not generally include a woman among their friends. Their relationshps to women are familial, marital or sexual. Friends in the non-West do not typically include parents, unlike the practice often met among Americans. Finally, friends are not typically shared as they habitually are among Americans — provided they are maintained in similar areas of activity. Friendship among non-Westerners is likely to be jealously guarded out of fear of losing or diluting it if other friends are brought into the relationship. As Foster has suggested, for much of Latin America true friendship is considered to be a scarce commodity (Foster, 1965, 298).

Personalization and Depersonalization

No one likes to be perceived as an object deprived of the human characteristics of a person and a member of the culture, even if a deviant member. Yet, what is personal for one person may not be for someone from another society. In each case, personalization conforms to cultural norms, social convention and to the individual's concept of the self. Personal treatment in American life includes use of the first name, recognition of biographical details and acknowledgement of specific acts, appearances, preferences and choices of the individual. Cultural models are given by salesmen and airline hostesses. Their pleasant smiles, feigned and innocuous invasions of privacy, "kidding" and swapping of personal experiences constitute stereotypes of personal behavior.

The latitude for personal expression differs from culture to culture. The Indian, for instance, is more inclined to become emotionally involved while discussing a topic than while discussing a colleague, the reverse of the American inclination. One group of Indians undergoing training in an American university were observed to load their words with emotion while discussing the problems of civil servants in the Indian Government. Personal comments were abstract and intellectual. When the topic of conversation veered toward the relationships among those in the group, it was eloquently proposed that the group select some other topic which would permit them to be **personal** and not allow the discussion to degenerate into discussing each other "and all that." This comment illustrates a view of personalism diametrically opposite to the American attitude.

Although the typical American tends to see himself as a unique individual with a private core inaccessible to others, as a rule he sees others as representatives of a class. They are not usually endowed with the same uniqueness reserved for the self. Hence, most Americans are relatively impartial and objective in the conduct of social relations in contrast to the personalized interactions found in most of the non-Western parts of the world. Examples are found in the paternal benevolence of the Japanese, the personal leadership of the Latin **caudillos**, and the nepotism endemic to non-Western countries. In each instance, Americans are likely to make a value judgment of "undesirable" since this is personalized interaction in areas where Americans are accustomed to depersonalized behavior.

"Personalization" is a desired quality for most Americans, implying good will, trust and acceptance of other people for what they are. In describing American social relations as "depersonalized" and those of the non-West as "personalized," an invidious comparison is not intended. Trust and good will, for example, need not be personalized. And, in turning to the personalized non-West, a chief characteristic of social relations is the distrust and suspicion repeatedly found among people. Personalization in social relations does not necessarily imply good will and trust.

This depersonalized behavior of Americans along with the values of achievement and equality, nurture competition as a means of social interaction. Each individual strives for his own personal goals. This disposition is found in personal interactions among individual American men where "friendly joshing," freely given advice, quick repartee and the "friendly suggestion" are subtle forms of competition. The individual who has the last word is "one up" on his companion, at least until the latter tells a better joke or in some way gives a twist to the competition that elevates him to the "one up" position. Although this sort of behavior in interpersonal relations may seem innocuous to Americans, such actions assume the proportions of competition and subtle coercion to other peoples (see Wax and Thomas, 1961).

Cooperation and "Fair-Play"

Competition among Americans occurs within the context of cooperation, for competition requires a considerable amount of coordination among individuals and groups. When the individual competes he is most likely at the same time to be cooperating. The typical American ability to cooperate is one of the advisor's most important assets overseas, for he may act as a catalyst to induce others to work together. One of the reasons Americans can do this — and they are well known for it — is that they do not commit themselves wholeheartedly to a group or organization. They pursue their own personal goals while cooperating with others who, likewise, pursue their own. They accept the goals of the group, but if their expectations are unfulfilled they then feel free to leave and join another group. This separation between membership in a group and personal objectives allows the individual to adjust his goals to those of other group members if it is necessary for carrying out joint action. To the American this compromise is practical, allowing him to achieve a benefit he could not attain on his own. Cooperation is given for the sake of action and it does not imply that the American yields his principles. He is in fact expressing a dominant assumption of American culture — the value of "doing." Principles, concepts and values are accepted only when they make a difference for activities in the world.

The importance of getting things done and a sense of urgency are often joined to elicit cooperation from members of a group who genuinely disagree with respect to either their principles or objectives. Thus, in many areas of

American life, a deadline or the prospect of future opportunities are frequently invoked in group deliberations as a means of overcoming individual differences. An appeal is made such as: "let's get the job done and then we can take care of these other problems." Or "go with us this time, and next time we'll go your way." Next time, however, frequently is displaced to the future, for Americans have a tendency to compromise on each issue. Everyone is expected to accommodate to the joint action, unlike the French who are more likely either not to compromise or to accommodate completely with each person having a turn at getting his own way. In this area of social cooperation Americans behave in a manner analogous to the "Dutch-treat."

It is apparent the American's preference for doing or for action may work against his individualism in a social setting. The necessity for compromise in cooperative action may undermine other values, principles or objectives of the individual. To insure that his adjustment or compromise is no more than necessary the American is likely to stress the means used to reach a group decision. In formal groups, for instance, he may be concerned with matters of agenda and procedure which tend to give some formal protection to the rights of the individual.

The American's abilities for cooperation and organization are not, as a rule, found abroad. The Latin, for instance, has a hard time adjusting his goals to those of the group or making a practical adjustment "to getting the job done"; this would be a compromise of principles. Likewise, in formal groups the Latin may see the raising of matters of agenda or other questions of group deliberation as avoiding the issue, whereas for the American it may be a matter of facilitating decisions fair to all. The concept of fairness is often invoked by the American in a situation where the Latin would understand the issues to implicate "dignity of man," "honor" or principles of belief. These concepts occur rarely in everyday behavior of Americans.

The value of fairness is not confined to face-to-face encounters in formal groups. It has widespread ramifications, often occurring as the value of "fair-play." The essence of it is not so much rules which ought to be followed as

> ...the inclusion of the other person's weakness inside the rule so that "fair-play" included in it a statement of relative strength of the opponents and it ceased to be fair to beat a weak opponent (Mead, 1965, 143).

The English notion of "fair-play" as modified in the United States is both an arbiter of personal relations among Americans and a motivating force. The American will stand up for his fair share and will be concerned with fairness toward others. He cannot initiate action if it involves aggression since he does not believe in beginning a fight. It becomes very important for him to be able to say "they started it," and then of course, "but we'll finish it." The significance of the value — accommodation to the weakness of another — is brought out in the mutual misunderstanding of the concept between Americans and members of other cultures. Americans cannot understand the deliberate and ruthless exploitation of a weak adversary by power and position in other cultures. On the other hand, to others the concept of fair-play may seem foolish, hypocritical and actually untranslatable into some languages — German, for instance (Mead, 1965, 143).

Need To Be Liked

Americans usually react to others as achievers and participants in certain activities rather than as whole persons. Hence, they usually establish a relationship on the basis of a common activity or interest, seldom comprehending the other as a total person. The usual view of the other is that of a potential response and it follows that the average American tries to anticipate the effects of his words and acts on others.* He envisions the desired responses and is likely to gear his actions accordingly. The characteristic of seeing others as responses is reflected in the emphasis on communication in interaction and in the great value placed on being liked. Overseas, this tendency is seen in the American's belief that the common people throughout the world will like him and he has often been fortunate in going to countries that were either neutral or favorably disposed toward him. It is difficult to say what would be the reactions of Americans if they had to work in places where they were not liked, for the American's esteem of others is based on their liking him (Linebarger, 1954, 384-385). This requirement makes it difficult for Americans to implement projects which require an "unpopular" phase. In the words of an English anthropologist, signs of friendship or love are

> ...a necessity for the American. He is insatiable in his demands for them, for any occasion on which they are withheld raises the gnawing doubt that maybe one is not lovable — not a success (Gorer, 1948, 133).

The need to be liked can clearly be a burden to the foreign student advisor who has services to render to which being liked or disliked is essentially irrelevant.

Signs of friendship, the glad handshake, the ready smile, the slap on the back, even some of the meaningless practices and phrases of business and advertising have become part of the normal way of behavior. Whenever the American is deliberately denied expressions of friendship or popularity, his reactions are confused, since he is denied one of the requirements for personal assurance. Social success for him often becomes a necessary part of achievement. Americans tend to judge their personal and social success by popularity — almost literally by the number of people who like them. It should be noted, however, that in this context to be liked does not mean one need like in return. To be liked or loved means simply that one is worthy of love (Gorer, 1948, 107). Popularity or friendship are both matters of social success and not the conditions for establishing warm, personal relationships.

---

*This emphasis on the other is different from the concern shown by the Oriental that his partner may say or do something which would lead him or his partner to lose face. The other person is seen as an entity although perhaps a worthless one. To the American the other person is quite often not an entity but a response to his own actions.

Specialization of Roles

A perspective on the individual has been maintained thus far in considering social relations in American culture. This point of view may be reversed for the purpose of looking back at the individual from the vantage point of social roles which American culture and all other cultures provide to integrate the individual into the society as a functioning member. These patterns of expectations and behavior are assumed by the individual according to his personal and social characteristics and the conditions under which he engages in a specific activity.

When the middle-class American male leaves his home to go to work, he leaves behind him his role as a family man and enters a world in which he is expected to make a clear separation between personal matters and his job. His work itself is separated into occupational roles. In American culture specialized roles are developed and filled with specialists who deal with specific functions and problems. The basic distinction of American organizations separates line from staff. Within this basic split, the development of specialized roles can proceed virtually unchecked. This happens especially, as one might expect, in business or the military whenever technical skills and complicated machinery are involved. However, the same tendency towards specialization of roles occurs in the realm of interpersonal relations, since the American's divisive or fragmenting attitude toward personality induces him to perceive others as achievers rather than as whole persons.

The separation of social and occupational roles and functions in American society does not correspond to the patterns found in other cultures. Many people, for instance, find it difficult to understand the American insistence on separating planning from operations. Specialization of roles in itself can also become a problem. Many Americans overseas complain that their opposite numbers do not delegate authority which perhaps may be interpreted to imply an absence of specialized roles; all functions are vested in the leader. This pattern of leadership is congruent with the concept of the whole person.

The typical American division of line and staff provides a contrast for the tendency in Latin America for each person in an organization to become a focus of power, which corresponds with the ascriptive orientation. The American idea of organizational channels of authority* are obscured, competing interests are set up and authority and power are diffused. Needless to say, occupational effectiveness is sacrificed. This kind of social organization is representative of the assumptions and values of Latin cultures and, hence, the North American style of social organization imposed on Latin America might not be effective. The American advisor overseas should be willing to adapt to local values and

---

*The ideal of the pyramid as the organizational form with a clear distinction between line and staff is no longer realized in many American organizations. This can be clearly seen in the military where the form of organization often is the diamond. The basic problem which the Army is facing and has not successfully solved is that the commanding officer must make decisions based on technical knowledge outside of his competence. In effect, "the expert" makes the decision and the necessity for his presence has inflated the number of staff and semi-command positions, giving the Army its diamond shape, rather than the classical pyramid (see Janowitz, 1959, 28-34).

perhaps experiment with an overlapping system of organization or some other form in which line positions and staff positions gradually merge.

Specialization of roles is not as extreme, generally, in American culture as in Japanese or, to a lesser degree, German culture. One role, however, that of the sick person, has become so specialized in American culture that he plays no useful part in society. If he remains on his feet he is praised for not allowing his illness to interfere with his work. If he is secluded in his home, friends and family members may pay a visit to him but there is a reluctance to intrude into his privacy. When sent to a hospital, the sick person becomes a case and, at best, a patient. His life is regulated according to the routines of the hospital, isolated from the mainstreams of life. He is deprived of a social role since his disease is defined as a physical condition.

This brief description of the role of the sick in American culture overlooks variations and shades of concern for the sick person as a social being, aspects which in other cultures provide the sick person with a social role. Thus when a man becomes ill he may serve as a catalyst to bring together members of the family and friends. There may even be social activities detrimental to the sick man's health and a sense of disappointment if he recovers before the appropriate social activities occur. Diseases are often considered to have social, ethical or magical meaning. An illness may be expiation for evil committed by an ancestor or a relative. The social basis of sickness may in some cultures be expressed by the belief that the illness is the result of the designs of a malevolent neighbor. Similar causes of disease also occur in American society but they are suppressed from consciousness, stripped of magical significance and called psychosomatic illness. The culture does not provide a social role for the sufferer.

The individual in American culture is presumed to have some control over disease. In characteristic fashion, the control usually refers to actions such as exercising, dieting and undergoing physical examinations that prevent the onset of disease. A similar individual factor is often found in other cultures although control by prevention is interpreted in a culturally relevant manner. Among the mestizo Colombians of Aritama (a pseudonym) there is a dimension to disease which appertains only to the individual and his will to overcome the evil that caused the illness. Sorcery expressing the hostility of a "neighbor" — who may be one's wife, sibling, relative or friend — is believed to be the real cause. The neighbor's ill will is feared more than the disease itself (Reichel-Dolmatoff, 1961, 209-311).

In the malevolent social climate of Aritama, the healthy individual

> ...is considered dangerous and is, therefore, an asocial element... To admit openly one is healthy is to challenge the social order. The usual and more acceptable attitude is one of complaints — of exagerrating the importance of any boil, cough or sneeze. To live 'suffering' (**sufriendo, padeciendo, aquantando**) is perhaps not a Christian virtue but, in Aritama, it is the best way to demonstrate that one is a well-meaning and harmless member of the community (Reichel-Dolmatoff, 1961, 313).

If the healthy individual is dangerous, then the sick person should enjoy a privileged social role in Aritama and such is the case.

A sick person occupies a privileged position which allows him to neglect obligations, reconcile himself with former enemies and receive favors without having to return them... A sick individual is never impure or evil, but is almost 'sacred' — sacred because world-controlling forces are involved — forces which have made him as an instrument and a victim in order to demonstrate their power (Reichel-Dolmatoff, 1961, 312).

The social role of the sick person in Aritama allows the individual to demonstrate his harmlessness and to gain prestige. His disease plays a prominent part in his life and his role of a sick person is functionally integrated into the social life in Aritama. Sickness and a social role for the sick person as found in this Colombian community provide a contrast to American culture which tends to isolate the sick person, depriving him of a functional social role.

3. PERCEPTION OF THE WORLD

Man and Nature

For the American, man's quality of humanness endows him with a value absent in all other forms of life: he is unique because of his soul. Man is clearly separate from nature and all other forms of life. Nature and the physical world are referred to as living but are conceived of as material and mechanistic.

To many cultures, on the other hand, man is just another form of life differing from others only in degree. Nature is alive and animistic. Animals and even inanimate objects have their own essence. Hence, in parts of the non-Western world no dividing line separates man from plants, rocks, rivers, mountains and valleys. Hindus and Buddhists believe life itself continues in endless cycles in which a soul can assume an infinity of forms. During one cycle the soul may inhabit the form of a man and in another take a different form — that of an animal perhaps, or an insect (Arensberg and Niehoff, 1964, 127-128).

A few agonistic references to India cannot begin to fill in the vast and intricate architecture of Indian thought regarding the world and man. The lofty tradition of India, extending 3,000 years and more into history, combines religion and philosophy into a way of thinking which shows a deep longing for infinity and for the unknown and a deep regard for Universal Being. Religion regulates the most minute details of everyday life (Nakamura, 1964, 157). An obvious example is found in the Hindu who refrains from raising cattle for food because the cow is sacred. The cultivation of plants has also been known to raise religious issues. Similar questions would be unlikely in Americans who see themselves as separate from animals and nature.

While religion in the United States is committed to the doctrine that man is evil by nature, most Americans are unlikely to give the concept much thought. More likely they will see man as a mixture of good and evil or a creature of his environment and experience. Most important, they will stress his ability to change. "Modern American religion inclines generally toward a remarkable perfectionism and optimism'' (Williams, 1961, 338) reflected in the deep conviction that man is perfectible — he can change and for the better. Furthermore, perfectibility can be approached through rational means; perhaps no people in history have believed so firmly as Americans in the ability of education to improve the individual. The belief in the perfectibility of man and in progress seems more characteristic of Americans than does the belief that man is innately evil. Doctrines of human nature are overshadowed by the view of man's ability to change his environment and to be affected by it. Man can change, improve himself, and it is his responsibility to do so.

Man's Relationship to Nature

The chief arena of American history has been nature (Boorstin, 1960, 175) rather than society, civilization or other peoples. The rich resources discovered as the new continent was settled invited the technological developments which have produced the material opulence of the society. Yet the economic and social development of America has been based squarely on values and assumptions of the people who settled it. The twofold category in American culture separating man and nature has been an important factor in the exploitative attitude toward nature which has contributed to the material richness of American society.

The dominant assumption in the United States is that nature and the physical world should be controlled in the service of man (see Kluckhohn and Strodtbeck, 1961). The American's formidable and sometimes reckless drive to control the physical world is perhaps unmatched as a dominant assumption in any other major society. It is best expressed by the engineer's approach to the world based on technology and applied to social spheres as ''social and human engineering.'' Americans have thrived in the well-controlled environment thus created. The natural laws assumed to underlie the physical world seem to be harnessed for producing material welfare and hence are at the service of man.

Alternative assumptions regarding the relationship between man and the world exist in American society and are dominant in other societies. One view prevalent in much of the Far East stresses the unity among all forms of life and inanimate objects. Man is considered to be integrated with nature and the physical world instead of in opposition to it. The assumption of integration is beautifully expressed in Japanese architecture. The form and lines of buildings and temples and the surrounding gardens appeal to the eye as a unity between the natural environment and the man-made structures. The observer easily passes from one environment to another without experiencing the discontinuity found in moving in and out of American structures which are usually built to dominate their surroundings.

The relationship between man and the world is subtle when described by a member of a culture where integration is the dominant assumption. The Japanese philosopher, Nishida, considers the world of historical actuality to consist of the subject and the environment (Tsunoda, et al., 1958, 868). (Subject seems to be very similar to our use of **man**, and environment to world.) The environment shapes the subject and is, in turn, shaped by the subject. Nishida apparently considers that the world of historical actuality is the result of a dialectical process between environment and subject. He describes occidental culture, on the whole, as moving from the environment to the subject. Movement of this kind yields a center of gravity in the environment rendering it subjective or, in our terms, nature and the physical world become the focus of cultural and historical interest. Oriental culture, in contrast, ''may perhaps be thought to move from subject to environment'' (Tsunoda **et al**., 1958, 869). The subject itself is negated and becomes environment — in our terms, a part of the natural world. Japanese culture represents a trend of Oriental culture. The essence of its spirit is to become one in things and events, to establish an identity between subject and world (Tsunoda, **et al**. 1958, 869).

The Western and the American view have led to objectivity about the world and the development of science and technology. The contrasting view has found expression in Far Eastern arts and religion although clearly Japan demonstrates that Oriental subjectivism does not prevent scientific and technological development as known in the West. Nishida identifies the additional quality in the Japanese which provided the impetus for economic and technological development as a congeniality towards man and a receptivity to foreign influences. Within this openness to man and the foreigner the ''Japanese spirit'' — unlike the Indian, for instance — moves from the universal principle to the particular event. Its concreteness, according to Nishida, affects the individual emotionally and transforms him ''from being that which is formed to that which forms'' (Tsunoda, **et al**., 1958, 872).

Nishida's analysis of Japanese and occidental culture provides some understanding of Japan's remarkable technical and economic development. The assumption that man is separate from the natural world and should control it has often been cited as underlying technological progress in the West. Yet Japan shows that a more integrated concept of man and nature can, in conjunction with other cultural characteristics, provide a basis for such development.

Not all peoples in the world share the assumptions of either controlling or integrating with the natural world. There are those who take a fatalistic attitude toward their environment, who feel overwhelmed by it. The Colombian mestizo considers nature to be dangerous and animated by the presence of spirits.

> Sun, moon and stars, wind and rain, heat and cold, light and shadow — all are believed to have occasionally harmful powers over body and mind. The cool air near the river or the reflected heat from rocks or trails, are thought to be dangerous, the same as the shadow of certain trees or the damp of the forest. Dangers are seen everywhere in nature and to try to understand them or to overcome them would be considered as foolishness (Reichel-Dolmatoff, 1961, 440).

The attitude of helplessness and mistrust is not confined to the physical environment but extends to the social and political orders.

These beliefs, and those of the people in cultures of poverty in many parts of the world, may be described as an assumption that man is subjugated by his environment (see Kluckhohn and Strodtbeck, 1961).

Materialism and Property

Guided by his stress on material things, the American overseas almost invariably judges the local society by his standards of material welfare defined in the broad sense of including physical comfort and health. He perceives his work to be congruent with his values and attempts to improve his health and promote the welfare of the local people, forgetting that the simple hygienic practices — sanitary toilets, vaccines, etc. — cannot be easily demonstrated to be effective in maintaining health. The American himself probably accepts them as part of his culture rather than on the basis of their demonstrated effectiveness. Quite often sophisticated observations and successive measurements over a period of time are required to make obvious the advantage of health measures.

The American stress on material things is associated with a belief in the inviolacy of private property. It has been asserted that this value is at the root of the Constitution and the American conception of democracy. The popular assumption that private property is inviolate has frequently led to friction between Americans and the citizens or bureaucracies of other nations, with subsequent repercussions at the highest levels of government. United States' relations with Latin countries have often been strained over the issue of private property, and danger to it is the usual reason advanced by Americans for intervention or threatened use of force. The Panama riots of 1964 provide an example of this sort of action and reaction. According to newspaper reports, American forces withheld fire until private property was threatened by the rioters. Also, negotiations between the United States and Latin American countries quite often revolve around the issue of private property for Americans versus human rights for the Latins (Northrop, 1946, 42-48; 94-98). The governments of these countries have sometimes expropriated American property, or even that of their own nationals, without what Americans feel to be valid reasons or fair recompense.

At the interpersonal level, many Americans also encounter difficulties in their dealings with non-Western persons who do not make a clear distinction between private and public property as the American understands it. Possession of property is affected by a person's position in society and his needs, as well as by other considerations. The simple distinction between private and public property becomes blurred by these factors.

Americans consider it almost a right to be materially well off and physically comfortable. They expect swift and convenient transportation — preferably controlled by themselves — a variety of clean and healthful foods and comfortable homes equipped with numerous labor-saving devices, certainly including central heating and hot water. The Government is expected to ensure that food and drug products meet acceptable standards and that appropriate public health measures are observed by all people and agencies whose activities can affect the public's welfare. Associated with the values of physical comfort and health is the acceptance of cleanliness as being nearly identical with health, if not with "Godliness."

Americans tend to project this complex of values, centering around comfort and material well-being, to other peoples. They assume that given the opportunity, everyone else would be just like themselves. Hence, they are disturbed by the sight of the rich churches of Latin America standing in the midst of poverty, the Buddhist meditating among the suffering and the rejection of American values throughout much of the world by men whose concepts of life are esthetic and spiritual.

Associated with material comfort is the American genius for devising and employing machines to provide efficiency and convenience in daily life. The American's faith in, and love for, machines goes abroad with him. American advisors and technicians exhibit a strong tendency to perceive their tasks as requiring the use of machinery so that the mechanical products of American factories have been shipped overseas in large numbers and placed in the hands of operators who do not have the skill or background to maintain them and who are often in countries where spare parts are not available. The machines soon become idle. Americans are usually correct in recognizing that machines can facilitate the tasks at hand, but they frequently overlook the fact that American machines and techniques of operation and maintenance are both integral parts of American technology. One cannot be exported without the other. Successful use of machinery requires a broad base of values and a social organization of roles to maintain, repair and operate the machines.

Progress

Interrelated with material property and material well-being is the value of **progress** which Americans often use to evaluate themselves and others. The concept is almost a cult in the United States and many Americans are surprised to learn that it is unknown and may be rejected by many in the non-Western world. It refers to a diffuse constellation of beliefs and attitudes lacking unitary value and assuming various forms. Mead has traced the origin of the concept in its broadest sense to the role of the parents in the United States (Mead, 1965, 133-136). In contrast to practices current in many parts of the world, American parents raise their own children, bravely assume responsibility for punishing them (which is actively avoided by parents in many cultures) and, thirdly

> ...act as if they themselves embodied all of the virtues which they are busy enjoining upon the child (Mead, 1965, 129).

At adolescence or thereabouts, the child usually realizes that the parents are not the paragons of virtue they pretended to be in accordance with the cultural norm. The child, often corrected and chastised by the parents, has a residual sense of guilt and, therefore, feels inadequate to fill the vacuum of goodness and virtue left by the downfall of the parents. Throughout the psychological crisis thus precipitated there usually remains the belief that there is something better than the parents and the self.

> And here, generation after generation, the belief in Progress is reborn in the minds of the young. Progress — the belief that there **is** something better than our own way of life — that our fumbling version of how men shall live with men here on earth, rests upon these very special mechanics in which parents first hold themselves up as good and their children learn the rare and beautiful faith that

there can be something better than oneself (Mead, 1965, 134-135).

Progress and Optimism in Contrast to Limited Good

Although "progress" in American society finds many expressions, it is perhaps most frequently associated with the technological control of the environment. Most Americans tend to believe the basic problems of the world are technological and their solution will bring about economic welfare. Economics is the final arbiter of the good and desirable. Progress, then, quite often means the achievement of physical comfort, good health (or the facilities for giving medical care), material possessions and a high standard of living. Throughout, there is an emphasis on convenience and the avoidance of danger and hardship. There is a distorted view of some of the difficult or unpleasant biological facts of life: birth, disease, physical abnormalities and death, the threat of which can be lessened through medical progress.

Bound up with the idea of progress in American culture is a feeling of general optimism towards the future. Most Americans feel that through their efforts a better future can be brought about which will not compromise the welfare and progress of others. There is enough for everyone — a belief which is valid for people living in a country with an expanding economy and rich resources. In contrast to this expansive view of the world, Foster has described the "Image of the Limited Good" which he suggests is widespread throughout peasant societies in the world.* He writes:

> By "Image of Limited Good," I mean that broad areas of peasant behavior are patterned in such fashion as to suggest that peasants view their social, economic and natural universe — their total environment — as one in which all of the desired things in life, such as land, wealth, health, friendship, love, manliness and honor, respect and status, power and influence, security and safety — **exist in finite quantity** and **are always in short supply**, as far as the peasant is concerned. Not only do these and other "good things" exist in finite and limited quantities, but in addition **there is no way directly within peasant power to increase** the available quantities. It is as if the obvious fact of land shortage in a densely populated area applied to all other desired things — not enough to go around. "Good," like land, is seen as inherent in nature — there to be divided and redivided if necessary, but not to be augmented (Foster, 1965, 296).

Since "Good" exists in a finite amount, an improvement in the position of an individual or family is a threat to the whole community for the gain must be a loss to someone else. The peasant's view of the natural and social world is usually limited to his immediate area; hence, the loss must be to someone in the community (Foster, 1965, 296-297). For this reason, there is often found an effort to conceal material gain or other improvement in an individual's or

---

*Peasant societies should not be equated to non-Western world; the expressions refers to those areas where population is dense and land holdings limited.

family's relative position in the peasant community. Or the individual or family may neutralize the improvement in the eyes of others by showing, usually in prescribed ways, there is no intention of using the improved position to the detriment of the community (Foster, 1965, 303).

In conclusion, progress is not a simple value. It is a process which reflects deep-seated characteristics of a cultural pattern. Those societies that do not have an appropriate temporal orientation, do not emphasize material things or lack the concept of a developing and hopeful future, are not likely to be swayed by the ideal.

Progress and the Concept of Time

The value of progress is integrated with other values and assumptions. It does not exist as an isolated belief. One of the most basic and systematic concepts underlying it is the concept of time. Progress is closely associated with the view that time is a flow in one direction, proceeding from the past, barely slowing for the present and rushing to the future. "Time moves fast." It is important for Americans to cope with this flow, for "you've got to keep up with the times."

This concept of time is eminently suited to a rational view of the world. One can distinguish various moments in time, note their relationship, and signal the relation by calling the preceding moment a cause and the next one an effect. Although over-simplified, the description identifies the American predilection for seeing the world in rather simple terms and, ideally, evoking a simple cause and effect sequence to explain events. On this firm foundation one can see the evolution of the dominant American belief in one's ability to master his environment.

Neither the concept of time nor belief in mastery of the environment is universal in the non-Western world. Indians conceive of time as cyclic, similar to the variant American concept of time manifested in predictions of weather and market fluctuations (see Bross, 1953, 38). Among the Chinese, too, time is cyclical, but it does not usually achieve the abstract qualities it attains in the West and among Indians (Granet, 1950, 86-113). Apparently the Chinese concept of time is more in the nature of an expansion of the present into both the past and the future with man occupying the center of the stage. Rather than existing as an abstract quality, each "cycle" or period of time has definite limits which coincide with the beginning and end of a unified train of events. Furthermore, temporal relationships are practically indistinguishable from spatial relationships: an event (or an object) may be contiguous with or separated from another before it or after it, but there is not necessarily a **causal** relationship between them. In effect, time does not provide the Chinese with the same rational means of explanation and prediction which the American and Western concept yields in material cause and effect. The Chinese demonstrates a much greater situation-centeredness and seeks an explanation for a specific happening in terms of other factors occurring at the same time as the event in question (certain events **naturally** go together) (Granet, 1950, 86-113). This view of time inclines the Chinese to integrate with the environment rather than master it and to adapt to a situation rather than change it.

Quantification

Another fundamental aspect of the American view lies in the stress placed on concreteness. But Americans do not require that they be able to touch, see, or in some other way personally encounter an object in order to establish concreteness. To the American the essential quality is measurability. The world to him is seen as having dimensions that can be quantified. Apparently there is not quality or experience that cannot be at least partially quantified — if only as first or last, least or most, or as having merely an arbitrarily assigned numerical value. Success and failure are measured by statistics; so is amount of work, ability, intelligence and performance. The quantification of the world and experience is deeply ingrained in the American. It is only with difficulty that he can understand the reactions of others to his practices. Yet, to some foreigners the description of, say, the Washington Monument in terms of statistics, devitalizes the experience of seeing it. Foreign students are often amazed at the value Americans seem to place on the streams of statistics they hear.

But quantification can also be disturbing or even threatening, as if the numbers used in some way reproduce the phenomenon described and destroy its reality. This idea is acted upon by the Kpelle of Liberia, who refrain from counting chickens or other domestic animals aloud in order to avoid some harm befalling them. The same practice has prevailed in other non-Western societies, including that of the Old Testament "where it was not considered proper to count people aloud lest some die" (Gay and Cole, 1967, 41).

The American use of statistics, such as the statement than an average family contains two and one-half members, impugns the dignity of the individual for some foreigners. A similar reaction may be elicited by a concept such as the man-year, which may include one or several men and extend from a fraction of a year to many years. Although such concepts as the man-year are considered practical and efficient by Americans and form the basis of planning in many American organizations, their measurability is not necessarily considered commendable by others for whom only a qualitative feeling, an impression, has the character of concreteness which Americans can evidently find in numbers and charts.

4. PERCEPTION OF THE SELF AND THE INDIVIDUAL

Dimensions of the Self

The concept of the individual self is an integral assumption of American culture so deeply ingrained that Americans ordinarily do not question it. They naturally assume each person has his own separate identity which should be recognized and stressed. Since this cultural assumption is implicit and outside of the awareness of Americans, the nature of self-identity is somewhat elusive. For Americans the main word associations to the self are **me** and **my** (Deese, 1965, 205), indicating the unexamined privacy of the concept. It is personal and presents one of the great dichotomies of American culture — the distinction between the self and other. The nature of the concept renders Americans incapable of understanding that in other cultures people may accept the distinction between self and other to be of the same kind and same magnitude as the difference between any two others. Most Indians, for instance, do not distinguish between the self of others and one's own self. "In India the tendency is not to regard another's self as an independent subject of action opposed to one's self" (Nakamura, 1964, 930).

A comparison of the "Who am I?" concept across cultures clarifies the American's tendency to see himself broadly as a human being of a particular sex. When a more specific identity is given, it is likely to be in terms of a social role (e.g., husband), identification with one's own generation and the achievements of the individual. This general perception of the self allows the American considerable freedom of choice in his actions, in contrast to narrower self-definitions of persons from other cultures.

The concept of self, therefore, has to be defined at a more abstract level to attain transcultural equivalence. The concept **self** implies the constellation of patterns of thinking, assumptions and values which supply to the person a sense of continuity in time and the ability to introspect. As an individual moves from event to event in his daily life he has a subjective feeling of the same person, the **me**, participating in each event and reflecting upon them. The concept of the self answers the question of what it is that underlies the awareness of continuity.

In many cultures, the individual may subscribe to the very general perception of the self held by Americans and, in addition, identify himself by constraints of birth and experience. Any one of these narrower factors may take precedence over the more general, ones used by Americans to define the identity of the individual. The self may be given an overly narrow definition by occupation (professor, soldier) or by family (a Smith, a Kennedy) (see Mead, 1963, 5) or the primary consideration in defining the self may be locale or ethnic group (a village, a particular mountain tribe in Vietnam). The narrower the perception of the self, the more precisely delineated will be the types of contact the individual will have with others, including people from other nations (Mead, 1963, 5). His social interactions will seem to be set and unchanging while his ability to be practical in choosing courses of action will seem limited.

When confronted with people who do not identify the self with the individual, Americans react with bewilderment, since the idea of the self not being located in the individual is culturally preposterous for most Americans. Yet the Japanese point of reference seems to be the network of obligations among the members of a group — the social nexus (see Nakamura, 1964, 409-417). The consequence of this definition of the self is that congeniality in social interaction becomes the predominant value. To varying degrees, a similar assumption pervades throughout the Orient. The stress on the relations among individuals rather than on the individual himself can be summarized in the concept of "face" with its concommitant ideas of "dignity," "prestige" and "respect." This concept is very confusing to American advisors for what they suggest as objective and practical courses of action may be rejected to spare someone's face. Where this concept prevails, attitudes and courses of action can best be understood as intending to preserve affiliations in groups and maintain congenial social relations and only secondarily to achieve certain goals which have a personal reference for the individuals involved. Foreign student advisors should keep this distinction in mind when advising Oriental students. Suggestions which from the perspective of the American advisor serve the self interest of the student may from the student's perspective be in conflict with his value system.

The concrete self-reference preferred by Americans becomes particularly important in work with counterparts overseas since it determines their outlook toward problems and actions. For example, a Bolivian insisted that Bolivia has one of the most advanced systems of social welfare in the world and refers to the country's constitution where social welfare provisions are spelled out. The informed American usually objects to the claim. Focusing on the individual, he points out the Bolivian worker does not receive the benefits his constitution provides; therefore, Bolivia does not have an advanced system of social welfare. To the Bolivian, the abstraction is important but to the American it is the involvement of the individual that matters. This difference in frame of reference is a recurrent issue between Americans and their counterparts.

Other abstract concepts of the self are even further removed from the self-reference of Americans, as is the case with the concept of the self as completely submerged in or subservient to the state. Duty and obligation are demanded of the individual who exists only for the state. The fanaticism and devotion to a cause or to country which this concept has generated among Germans and others are usually little understood by Americans, who conceive of the state as a collectivity which exists to serve them and their relationship to it as one of rights. In the American view, the state assures the individual his freedom and rights, grants him security and protection, but respects his autonomy by not interfering in his life. That this view does not always correspond with reality does not lessen its significance as a view.

Individualism and Individuality

The American stress on the individual as a concrete point of reference begins at a very early age when the American child is encouraged to be autonomous. The self-centeredness of the child is seldom questioned. It is implicitly accepted that each child or person should be encouraged to decide for himself, develop his own opinions, solve his own problems, have his own things and, in general, learn to view the world from the point of view of the self. The American is not expected to bow to the wishes of authority, be it vested in family, traditions or some organization. A recent study of families in an Appalachian poverty area ascribed the lack of economic development there to the fact that the families did not allow their children to challenge the authority of their parents — as most American families do. The children therefore grew up without the ability to challenge or change the economic situation in which they found themselves.

This untrammeled freedom of choice and self autonomy does not exist in a social vacuum. Social control and even a form of social coercion is found in the nebulous but imperative expectation the individual will choose as everyone else wants him to. As Florence Kluckhohn has put it, the individual is "'free to be like everyone else'" (F. Kluckhohn and Strodtbeck, 1961, 23). Thus, the stress on the individual as a concrete point of reference is consummated in the value of individualism.

The pressures on the individual are usually informal since he is assumed to be a free agent. If he conforms to the pressures from his group, family or associates, he belongs. If he chooses to deviate from the norms expected of him then he runs against the American intolerance of "rate-busters," "nonconformists," etc. He fails to receive the fruits of approval, esteem and popularity which are so important in American culture. One observer has gone so far as to say success in American life is not, as many believe, an end in itself. It is pursued for

> ...social acceptance — not for pleasure or power, but for admiration, love and even self-respect (Kaplan, 1958, 71).

The value of **individualism** as found among Americans is quite different from a stress on individuality (see F. Kluckhohn and Strodtbeck, 1961, 23-24). Americans overseas, valuing individualism, are often surprised to find persons who evince strong personality, personal convictions and idiosyncratic behavior. These persons seem to be individualists in every sense of the word and yet live in cultures where authority (usually family) or tradition exercise considerable control over the person. The contradiction is only apparent. In some cultures where the individual is subject to the norms of his family or tradition he is allowed considerable room to cultivate individuality, as long as these do not interfere with his obligations to family or tradition. The individualism of American culture does not prescribe specific obligations for the individual but, at the same time, it affords much less freedom for self expression.

In American culture, individualism has emphasized the individual while accepting affiliations within a group. Americans are not and probably have never been independent persons relishing their individuality. Not even the frontiersman fulfills the image. Daniel Boorstin remarks "...of all American myths, none is stronger than that of the loner moving west, across the land. ...The pioneering spirit, we are often told, is a synonym for 'individualism'" (Boorstin, 1965, 51). But Boorstin challenges the myth of this rugged individualist who colonized the eastern seaboard and then conquered the West. He marshalls evidence to show it was casual informal groups, readily formed and readily dissolved, which colonized the wilderness and stamped the American character from the beginning with its group consciousness.

Myths of the American frontier which have persisted until recent years stress a number of values which are invoked indiscriminately and, hence, are not descriptive of behavior. Nevertheless, these cultural norms carry considerable emotional impact. One of the most important of these is **self-reliance**, which in its pure form no longer makes sense in the complex technological culture of the United States. The fierce **self-reliance** advocated by Emerson has yielded to a search for **autonomy, self-actualization** and **personal growth**. The emphasis resides in the self but there is no longer the driving aspiration for independence of the individual. We shall refer to these various constellations of assumptions and values as **self-reliance**, a cultural norm which persists in American society as a potent focus for the emotions and motivations of Americans. To the same extent that self-reliance is supposedly sought, its opposite, dependence, is avoided. Since Americans can envisage few fates worse than to be dependent, self-reliance is a powerful incentive and it is one Americans themselves may inappropriately employ to motivate people overseas. Although self-reliance is out-of-date in the United States, the American often functions best as the member of an organization and advisors overseas are often too quick to fall back on the frontiersman's ideals and hold at fault the foreigner who shows no liking for self-reliance.

The meaning of the value is neither translatable nor self-evident in other cultures. For example, in the Spanish of Latin America, self-reliance is translated as "independence" and carries the suggestion of political and social freedom as well as the implication of solitary action, but the idea of the self as the source and sole limiting factor is missing. These ideas are not congenial to the Latin who has a strong attachment to his family and immediate group. Dependence is not deplored by him as it is by Americans. And among the Chinese, dependence on others is desirable for it strengthens the relationship among people. Chinese parents, for instance, take pride in being dependent on their children and supported by them in a manner to which they are unaccustomed. It is apparent, then, the American advisor who appeals to self-reliance is talking against the current of values in the non-Western world where relations to others, including dependence, take primacy over self-reliance.

Self-Motivation

Unlike other societies, American culture does not attribute particular meaning to place of birth, family, occupation, politics or the other ascriptive considerations which can be used to define the self. The existence of the individual is a matter of chance with no significance attached to origin or destiny. Self-definition is determined primarily by personal achievement. The individual himself should set his own goals and then make up his own mind on how to pursue them. Motivation, in the sense of long-range goals, as well as motivation for a specific and immediate task, should originate with the person.

A consequence of the American's identity is that his self-concept usually does not merge with a group. He maintains a separate sense of individuality. To him, any group ranging from a small one to the nation is a collection of individuals. He requires that his individuality be recognized by his being given opportunities to express his opinion and take part in group decisions, since as a member of a group he is presumably pursuing his own self-interest. He does not like to get lost in or to become deeply identified with great causes and large groups. With Americans, there is always some danger, it has been said, that a given war (Vietnam?) or a cause (the United Nations?) runs the risk of suddenly seeming to be unnecessary (see Williams, 1954, 123).

The idea of self-motivation naturally accompanies an identification of the self with a specific individual. Americans tend to dislike motives originating in others which are then applied to them. They strongly reject motivation in the form of orders, injunctions and threats emanating from authority. Probably it is this dislike which makes Americans anti-militaristic rather than a rejection of fighting or violence (Gorer, 1948, 39). The overt authority of the military, based upon enforced discipline and the prerogatives of rank which derive from status rather than achievement, is repugnant to the typical American. The American military, despite its necessarily ascriptive orientation, is characteristically American in its de-emphasis on the power and privileges of rank — in marked contrast to the military in most other countries.

The American concept of the self and self-motivation causes stress both in American institutions and in the general life-style prevalent in the United States. If coercion is disapproved and authority rejected, how do Americans manage to coordinate their lives and activities? The answer is through persuasion. The desire to act according to the wishes of others is instilled in the individual by means of examples, incentives and subtle hints of failure. It is perhaps the threat of failure which contributes the most to persuasion and provides the basis for appeals to self-interest and reason. Coercion, when necessary, should be applied informally so that the power of authority is masked. If possible, the individual is allowed to maintain the illusion that what he is compelled to do was decided by himself in his self-interest. In the final analysis, it is not the conformity and the inevitability of authority which Americans dislike, but the assault upon the self as the subjective and private core of the individual.

Although Americans tend to reject overt authority when it is exercised over people, they accept authority employed over things and processes. Control over natural resources, goods, services, money, etc. is considered either natural or desirable (Gorer, 1948, 40-41). This view is well adapted to the achievement motivation of the American. But emphasis on achievement and its corresponding disregard for the person produces a side effect on the individual: he is made to feel he is inherently replaceable and his associates, however much he may value them, are also replaceable. This feeling spurs the American on to greater achievement (see Henry, 1963, 29).

By defining people according to achievement, Americans can fragment their own personality or that of the other person. An American does not have to accept the other person in totality to be able to work with him; he may disapprove of the politics, hobbies or personal life of an associate with whom he can work effectively. It is this trait of seeing others fragmented that provides the American with his ability to cooperate. An individual with ascriptive motivation, however, tends to react to others as total or whole persons. Frequently, he cannot work with or cooperate with a person of different religion, belief or ethical code, since there is a total rejection of the other person. This tendency to accept or reject the person completely is at the root of the observation that Americans overseas have to watch every act, for what the American does away from work affects the attitude of his associates toward him.

One very important consequence of the American tendency to view people in fragments is that actions, thoughts and intents are separately evaluated. Legally, the individual cannot be held liable for harboring undesirable thoughts. On the other hand, demonstration of desirable intentions is grounds for excusing an undesirable action. In parts of the non-West, however, there is no clear differentiation of this kind within the personality. Thus, indication of "wrong thoughts" is grounds for censure even though undesirable actions may not result. And actions, if wrong, are very difficult to overcome. They are not forgotten, regardless of the intentions behind them.

The synthesis of action, thought, feeling and intent of the individual is illustrated by a power struggle within the Chinese Communist Party in 1954 (Ravenholt, 1964, 175-184). Two members of the central authority of Communist China, Kao Kang and Jao Shu-shih, were ousted from power and deprived of all titles and authority. The two men were accused of various "crimes." The accusations against Kao Kang were that his crimes were "substantially those of violating basic tenets" (Ravenholt, 1964, 177). The charges were substantiated by incidents occurring during the previous 20 years, a period during which Kao Kang had exercised his greatest power and influence. Essentially, Kao Kang was confronted with his whole history with no effort made to isolate significant criminal actions. The whole man was judged. The same strategy was employed against Jao Shu-shih, who was accused of defiant acts, crimes of attitude and crimes in the "sphere of thought." In his case, as in Kao Kang's, there was little if any distinction made among actions, intentions and "spheres of thought" (see Ravenholt, 1964, 175-184).

Resistance to Systems of Thought

The American is a pragmatist. He acts in a way that gets things done. If an idea works he uses it. That several of his ideas or values may contradict one another does not bother him. Nor does inconsistency in living up to a value. Coherent personal philosophies and systematic ideologies are both exceptionally rare in American culture. Values are traditionally given specific applications and their contradictions are ignored or rationalized. This social process has been called "situational specification of generalized values" (Williams, 1964, 27).

> ...the implications of certain initially given values have been explored in a great variety of specific social contexts, resulting in numerous modifications and restrictions in application. Thus, "freedom" is now felt to be compatible with compulsory vaccination, compulsory school attendance and peacetime military conscription... (Williams, 1964, 27).

The burden of inequality placed upon the Negro in the United States has been the outstanding cultural contradiction in American history. In an attempt to make it compatible with the assumption that all men are equal, the humanness of the Negro was denied by many. A more sophisticated rationalization, with tinges of both politics and logic, was the "separate but equal" doctrine which, for many decades, provided the basis for segregation. At a more personal, emotional level, many whites often simply acted as though Negroes just did not exist.

A similar reluctance to spawn an ideology or a philosophy exists at a more strictly political level in the United States. Thus, Americans are likely to ignore or deny the implications for "the free enterprise system" (as close to a political-economic philosophy as most get) of Social Security, TVA, the GI Bill of Rights, minimum wage laws and governmental assistance to agriculture, oil interests and the airlines. Each one of these practices and others with similar implications had to be fought out in its own terms, since TVA does not establish a precedent for the development of the Columbia River basin and Social

Security does not predispose to Medicare. These are somewhat general statements requiring considerable reservations. But they do indicate one deeply imbued cultural value: the American resists systems of thought which lose sight of the individual. The many elements of governmental responsibility and care for the individual are not usually unified into a system of ideology (see Perry, 1949). Americans typically cling to the ideal of individual enterprise, a belief which maintains the self-identity intact. The aversion to a coherent system of thought is again reflected in the traditional organization of political parties. Thus, the two major parties, the Democrats and the Republicans, are more aptly described as instrumentalities for securing political power, rather than as representatives of ideological beliefs.

> ...For the function of a political party in this country is not to preside over a philosophical debate but to control and direct the struggle for power...(Reston, 1965).

The American's distrust of systems of thought often leads him to underestimate the impact that a coherent, comprehensive ideology and philosophy such as Communism can have on other peoples whose thinking does not revolve around the individual. It provides an explanation of socio-economic conditions, makes projections of the future and, perhaps most important of all, provides a plan of action for the person as a member of a class rather than as an individual. Equally the American may overestimate the attractiveness of the self-oriented, pragmatic non-ideology sometimes called "Americanism."

Cultural Change

A searching look at any aspect of American culture readily brings the self to the surface as a unifying concept. The self provides a perspective in thinking, a direction for activity, a source of motivation, a locus in decision-making and a limit to group involvement. Although personality is fragmented to accommodate to the demands of the culture, the identity of the individual is held together by the self. Providing continuity for the individual, the self furnishes the quantum of the culture. All messages, transactions and activities in life which yield an impact upon Americans must be translated into the language of the self. Stated differently, communication with Americans hinges on the ability to evoke their self-interest and involvement, at least vicariously.

This concept of the self as the quantum of the culture draws together various strands of activity and belief in American culture and deeply affects its values and assumptions. The salience of the self and of the individual in the cultural patterns, however, does not necessarily mean that the individual is valued. We have seen that the individual is depersonalized and that individuality is not cultivated in American culture. The self as the quantum of the culture merely implies that the concept is a necessary and concrete point of reference. For instance, the concepts of dignity and human nature, which are so important for Latins, become literary and imprecise ideas in the United States. They are too abstract for Americans to employ them confidently as everyday ideas. If they are used at all they are more likely to be rendered as self-respect, needs and goals. In each instance a more concrete and self-referring term is used; Americans are usually apologetic when they refer to concepts that do not have a clear reference to the quantum — the individual as a self.

Yet there is a rebellion going on today against this fundamental concept. Young people in particular have deplored the depersonalized and alienating aspects of the American self. For these reasons, the concept appears to present an excellent focal point for an examination of cultural change.

There is no existing society which has institutionalized change to the degree of American culture. A description of the United States cannot pretend to completeness without at least passing mention of it. Yet the very centrality of change for Americans and the enthusiasm with which it has been embraced makes it a subject difficult to consider. American culture itself provides at least three obstacles to an appraisal of change.

In visiting a new area of the country, the visitor is usually provided with a description of "how much things have changed." The visitor himself frequently asks for this information implicitly, since the American perception of actuality depends on the recognition of change. Without a before-and-after comparison Americans are relatively impervious to their environment. Change and novelty are necessary features of things in American life, and for both the mass media and the individual they become labels for preferences. Under these circumstances it is difficult to judge innovation in American culture, since each American event or phenomenon is accompanied by the clamor of immediate impact and meaning.

A second obstacle is more subtle; it can be illustrated with the concept of the self. All roads in the culture lead to the quantum, which is irreducible but must remain private, vague and ambiguous. Otherwise, the self-concept would contradict the fragmentation of personality and the emphasis on achievement. These qualities in the self, existing detached from origins and uncommitted to any destiny, invite a search for meaning. Each generation of Americans is committed to the re-discovery of the self and to claiming it as its own invention. To re-enforce the uniqueness of the discovery, it becomes necessary to create social identities by means of a new youth culture. The development and exploration of the self takes places in the cultural islands created.

The phenomenon of self-discovery is a description of a complex cultural and social phenomenon. Nevertheless, it can be argued that there is an ambiguity in American culture with respect to assumptions and values about the self, progress, and good and evil — to mention three instances — which create the conditions for perpetual rediscovery by each generation and each interest group. Tradition and education do not clarify or define these cultural ambiguities; instead, they encourage their investigation.

A third obstacle exists to the isolation of change in the society. Personality is too frequently assumed to remain relatively stable over the human life span. Individuals vary, however, as they pass into adolescence, advance into maturity and, finally attain old age. Genuine changes in culture that have been claimed by youth in the decades of the sixties have to be separated from the passage through a stage of **being** which seems to be the path traveled by all youth.

While keeping in mind the above reservations regarding the diagnosis of change in society, we may note the frequency with which the increasing tendency toward organization and depersonalization in American life has been pointed out since the Second World War. The typical American is apparently now more willing to place himself in the hands of the government or of an organization, accepting their policies and goals as his own, than was the American of a generation ago.

> Strictly personal values have receded in importance at the expense of more publicly standardized "group values" whether those of an organization, a community, social class, profession, a minority or an interest group (C. Kluckhohn, 1958, 105).

The import of this change is that the influence of organizations and groups, which historically was mediated by informal pressures masked as public approval, is becoming more explicit among middle-class Americans. The great "They say..." is becoming increasingly identified as the voice of the Government or of some organization.

Along with the change in the American's willingness to immerse himself in a group, there have been similar changes in other values associated with the self-identity. Variations from the dominant value have become more prominent. The concept of freedom in American culture has been traditionally centered in the individual's freedom of choice. The individual defined government as guaranteeing to him certain rights rather than demanding obligations. Political institutions were kept to a minimum and drew their strength from the local scene. Throughout American history, and particularly since the 1930's, the position of the central Government has strengthened. Paralleling this development, there has been a general centralization and increased organization in several areas of American life: government, business, labor, education and recreation. The traditional American concept of freedom as individual choice has undergone considerable change.

As a result the personal outlook of Americans as well as the manner in which their activities are organized have become less personal. The boundaries of the quantum have become blurred with the loss of distinctiveness between one individual and others. The changes in the American self-concept have not been so much in the growth of a general social consciousness as in the increased openness of the self to special groups and causes.

The breakdown of boundaries can be perceived in innumerable areas of American life. An obvious change has occurred in the traditional insistence on sexual differences between male and female. The body image, dress, appearance and behavior separating the two sexes can now be described among young people on a continuum of minimal differences. A breakdown in the boundaries defining obscenity in the mass media and art and in behavior has also taken place.

Both Negroes and young people in American society show an increasing obliteration of the boundaries which define individualism and, hence, the quantum of the culture. The Negro, in particular, has consciously attempted to establish a self which includes the attribute of "blackness." The identity is an ethnic one, that is, a group identification. For Negroes, youths, and other segments of the society, conclusions are now reached through concrete association rather than more abstract processes of thinking (Glenn, 1969). The abstract boundaries around concepts have yielded to perceived social and cultural necessities. Education, for instance, can no longer be easily distinguished from social action; the demand for relevance in education obscures the difference.

The changes in American values and assumptions do not necessarily represent major changes, since they are concentrated in a small segment of the society. All of the factors, however, contribute to what may be a major development in American culture. The last 25 years suggest the main lines of a new and unfolding American drama.

For generations, the American mind was transfixed by the frontier and the conquest of the West. As we have noted, the arena of American history has been nature, and the antagonist, the Indian and the wilderness. The Western movie and novel captured the epic struggle of man against nature and "the savage." The experience gave birth to a feeling of American distinctiveness from the remainder of the world. This feeling of uniqueness, which prevailed during the 19th century, began to ebb in the 20th century as the United States attained the stature of a world power. "This declining sense of American uniqueness is the great trauma of the American mind in the last half-century" (Boorstin, 1960, 121). The insularity of the twenties and thirties began to give way to a receptivity to foreign influences. After World War II, foreign beliefs and practices, particularly if they appeared exotic and mystical to the American mind, replaced the past, and the struggle between "Communism" and democracy replaced the struggle between the frontiersman and the Indian symbolic of a simpler age. Incredible events which formerly were acceptable only when reported from Peshawar or some other remote place in the world became easily believable when attributed to the United States. Yet unconsciously American emotions which had been projected at foreign peoples and countries were redirected toward the American South, which became the subterranean field of American culture. It is on this familiar ground that matters of conscience and guilt for American culture were going to be fought out. The external antagonists began to crumble. The monolithic invention of Communism, strong in the fifties, provided the sole binding factor in an otherwise disjointed foreign policy. By the late 1960's, it was no longer able to provide direction and purpose to American national life. The antagonists of the culture were increasingly identified as members of the society.

The inward look, so characteristic of America now, represents a change in the American self-concept. It establishes a tension within the society and within the self which replaces the epic struggle between man and nature; it confronts Americans with a concept of evil which replaces failure to achieve and a capability for violence which overshadows the ethic of work. The patterns of thinking are more concrete, associative and intuitive. The values and assumptions no longer reflect the pursuit of success through change and achievement; instead, they reveal a concern with love, identity and power. It is quite clear that the arena of American culture is no longer nature, but society itself. This may be a major new direction in American culture.

Part VI
APPLICATIONS

The American advisor overseas is deprived of the many familiar guide-posts of his own culture which allow him to act without thinking. The result is that in an overseas setting each simple act may require planning and a decision. For example, he may not know when to shake hands or when to nod his head; he may not realize when he should ask a question, express an opinion, or maintain silence. He may blunder in the techniques that he uses in giving advice, and he may create awkward if not disastrous social situations by his ignorance of the "proper channels of communication."

The deepest shock to the advisor may come when he has penetrated into the world of work.

> Here he sees what looks like familiar bureaucratic structures and technological systems but the way they actually function is confusing. He meets people with professional training similar to his own but who do not always act in their work role as expected — yet he depends on them for getting the job done. Frustration becomes part of his everyday language if he finds no way to achieve fuller understandings of why things which look alike do not perform as they are supposed to (Useem, **et al**. 1963, 179).

When the strangeness of life in a foreign country leads to uncertainty, the individual's own cultural pattern intrudes with tentative interpretations to dispel the ambiguity created by the unusual behavior of foreigners. The individual is not likely to suspend judgment and action until he fully understands the strange ways, since his own assumptions, values and habits are seen as normal, while he is likely to regard those of another culture as strange, undesirable, unnatural or immoral.*

In considering his own cultural assumptions and values as natural, the advisor creates one of the most stubborn obstacles to cross-cultural cooperation. The problem is particularly accentuated when the individual advisor works with foreigners in the context of his own familiar organization, since these conditions provide him with little if any incentive to recognize the cultural biases of his behavior and to question the objectivity of his actions. An understanding of the biases and underlying predispositions of American culture should aid the advisor in ridding himself of the belief that his own assumptions and values should be the norm for all peoples. This change in attitude does not mean, of course, that the American advisor should discard his own culture even if it were possible for him to do so, or even that he should value it less highly, but it should predispose him to perceive both his own

---

*The presumed superiority of one's own cultural pattern is, of course, characteristic not only of Americans, but of most peoples of the world.

behavior and that of his counterparts more objectively. One of the consequences of the advisor's objectivity should be his ability to avoid many types of misunderstandings frequently arising because of the differences between American cultural patterns and those of the counterparts.

The misunderstanding caused by the incongruity between cultural patterns is specific to actual events; the description of each example requires the simultaneous employment of several, if not all, of the components. They are the tools of analysis which will be used to analyze concrete examples from the field and from American settings. In reporting the case studies, the actual facts will be interwoven with the explanations to present a more coherent picture.

The stated purpose of this book is to clarify misunderstandings and problems which emerge among people because of cross-cultural differences — differences in patterns of thinking, assumptions and values — between American advisors and their counterparts. These misunderstandings and problems have often been mentioned in the process of illustrating American and non-Western assumptions and values. Hence, the present section differs from those preceding only in presenting in greater depth actual problems encountered overseas and in the United States.

1. PATTERNS OF THINKING AND SOCIAL CONFLICT

Most Americans incline toward the belief that sufficient time, effort and skill will insure success in communication, which becomes almost synonymous with agreeing. Thus, technical matters related to the process of communication assume the greatest importance among Americans, while matters of substantive differences which cannot be bridged by skillful communication receive minimal attention. Also ignored are the purely stylistic matters of patterns of thinking and their effect on communication. The two incidents reported below draw attention to neglected aspects of thinking and show how these factors are usually considered at the social, political or some other level. Their roots in culture are ordinarily disregarded.

A small seminar group was engaged in discussing the American participation in the war in Vietnam. A member of the class deplored the fact that the casualty rate of American forces was approaching 40,000 killed. Several other members of the class agreed it was a national tragedy. The instructor in the class then pointed out that the war in Vietnam had to be considered along with other factors. Fifty thousand Americans were killed on the highways each year, whereas in Vietnam nine years of war had not equaled the rate of highway slaughter for one year. Other members of the class then brought into the discussion other aspects of technological society that deeply affect human welfare, such as air pollution in the cities.

Most of the students in the class seemed to concur with the direction of the discussion. There were nodding of heads and expressions of agreement as various consequences of modern life were equated with the effects for Americans of the Vietnam war. One student, however, took an emotional exception to the comments which had been made. She stated she could not understand the comment about highway fatalities and saw no connection between that statistic and the casualties in Vietnam. She asserted that when one drives a car there is no intention to harm others but in war the intent is to kill.

It became clear that a polarity had developed in the class discussion. The lines between the one student and the rest of the seminar group were drawn and remained firm until the end of the session. With the lapse of time until the next session, one week later, it became apparent that the discussants in the seminar were observing two different styles of thinking. In one case, the war in Vietnam was judged strictly in terms of its consequences, the casualty rate; therefore, it was appropriate to compare it with other similar consequences, that is, fatalities on the highway. The one dissident student, however, insisted the terms of comparison must include a value, in her words: "intent." The intent or the value made the difference for her and not the consequences. The majority of the students in the class were employing a comparative judgment, while the lone dissident insisted on an absolute judgment; in her case, the intent of the actions. Since the students were in general agreement regarding the war in Vietnam, it was the style of the discussion, the two ways of evaluating, which caused the breakdown in communication.

The incident is important for showing the impact of styles of thinking and suggesting how an impasse in this area is misinterpreted and usually projected to the social or another level of human interaction. This latter consequence is clear in the incident reported below:

About 20 American executives were brought together to participate in a training program. The managers were members of a large American corporation; they had been drawn from the northeastern part of the United States. One or two had been hired from other companies and one member of the group was a foreigner recently come from abroad. They were brought together for a few days to become acquainted with each other before assuming the functions of the policy-making group of a new plant built by the corporation in the southern part of the United States. For one of their training sessions they had read a recent book on management techniques. During the session they discussed its contents so as to clarify their own policies on management.

As the discussion progressed, the group quickly became polarized. The majority of the American managers occupied one position and a few were silent, while the foreign engineer — highly trained and experienced — occupied an opposite position in the discussion. As the managers talked, their language became more violent and the comments more personal. The Americans exhibited an operational pattern of thinking. It is partly inductive in nature but its main feature is that the language used is rather vague. It anticipates consequences and looks for criteria of measurement. Often encountered are words and phrases such as "cost-benefit," "productivity," "making a profit," "making the best use of your time," "change," etc. The quality of the thinking is seen in the language used; it implies a projection to the future, its consequences, and suggests the quality of efficiency. Cost-benefit and profit are used as criteria for the success on the job.

To an outsider the discussion would have made very little sense. The managers were making comments based on terms and ideas which were implicit and intuitive operating principles. They were agreeing on principles and policies and rehearsing a language that described the management-climate of their company. They were not generating policy or principles of leadership. From the outsider's point of view, their thinking was vague and ambiguous.

The comments made by the non-American engineer were quite different. Speaking perfect English, he frequently insisted he did not understand what the Americans were talking about. His words suggested a different level of thought; he repeatedly emphasized the necessity of knowing the specific context in which a given working situation or problem had arisen. He emphasized his own experience as an engineer and how, out of these experiences, he had been able to develop rules-of-thumb or criteria which he would apply to new situations as they arose. He felt it was relatively futile to attempt to predict the highly general and vague possibilities which the managers might encounter in their new plant; these were meaningless issues to him.

In brief, we may say the Americans basically were inductive but at a relatively general or operational level, and their thinking was based on the anticipation of consequences realistic and imagined. In contrast, the thinking pattern of the non-American engineer tended to run from the abstract to the concrete. He wanted rather specific instances — the context, as he called it, or the environment. At the same time he searched for principles which were relatively free of the contingencies of the moment and for guidance from his own experience. He was very reluctant to engage in free speculations without knowledge of the situation.

In summary, the general attitude of the non-American engineer was that the Americans were not very clear thinkers and really did not know what they were talking about. The concern with generalities which might or might not come about, their involvement with the obvious and their vagueness deserved little attention. The Americans' attitudes were quite different as they claimed the engineer was obnoxious, antagonistic and attempting to disrupt the harmony and workings of the group. Neither the foreign engineer nor his American colleagues recognized the source of their difficulty. The cultural differences in patterns of thinking were readily projected to personal and unfavorable characteristics of individuals, who were assigned disruptive social motives.

2. THE CAPITAL SELF

It was stated earlier that the self in Indian culture possesses an objectivity that does not differentiate between the self and the other. The private and subjective self — separate from every other self — is an American concept which the Indian would regard as an illusionary appearance occurring in the external world (Nakamura, 1964, 93). The American view of the self, as well as variants found in other parts of the Western world, is considered to have appeared in the West at the beginning of the modern age. People, however, who employ a historical reserve of meaning find the roots of their values and assumptions in traditions and norms preceding the present era.

Styles of establishing meaning and the concept of the self are fundamental characteristics of the individual's culture which arise in the most commonplace events of daily life. Most people are oblivious to their cultural implications, since much of culture is not available to awareness. It is relatively rare to encounter someone who has experienced cultural differences and who at the same time is articulate about them. Such is the case of M.M., a Greek foreign student, described below, who is pursuing graduate studies at an American university.

M.M. came to the United States with impressive academic credentials — a degree in law and three published books, two in sociology and one in the classics. When M.M. discussed his experiences with Americans, he had been in the United States for about one and a half years. His speech was marked by a heavy accent and he occasionally searched for a word, but his command of English was firm. His ability with grammar and English style permitted him to function at any academic level in an American university.

When M.M. arrived in the United States he spoke Greek, German and French, but not English. He joined a class to learn it and, one day, while attending class, he was struck by the phrases which the instructor placed on the board:

I am; you are; he is; etc.

I, the vertical pronoun, was capitalized, while the others were not. He made this observation to the teacher and remarked that English is the only language that uses the capital with the pronoun. The instructor was taken aback by M.M.'s reaction to this commonplace feature of the language. To M.M. the capital **I** reflected the individualistic element in English and in native speakers of the language.

M.M.'s observation on the pronoun was extended to other experiences which to him also reflected the qualities of the ''self'' concept in American life. He was surprised by a grandmother's remark, ''I will buy a dress for her.'' The reference ''her'' was to a granddaughter. In the phrase, M.M. perceived an inordinate emphasis on the difference between the grandmother and the granddaughter as though they were two separate and equal beings without any distinctions in age, position or status. The separateness and subjectivity of the implied concepts of the self and the individual did not reflect the sociological variables which for M.M. would define the individual. Furthermore, the phrase did not show the bond between the two persons. M.M. felt he would be more at ease with expressions implying the belongingness common to the grandmother and the granddaughter — references to the girl as ''my granddaughter'' rather than ''her.'' The emphasis on the separateness of the two persons fails to reflect the ''moral'' act which for M.M. may be interpreted as ''socially responsible'' or ''humanistic.'' In both the Greek language and culture there is a structural association between the ''I'' and the ''you.'' The relationship is neither casual nor informal. Instead, it refers to abstract qualities of responsibilities, loyalties and duties of the persons involved. In Greek to communicate (''talk'') is to search for truth by means of language. M.M. perceives talk among Americans as a way of establishing association among persons.

A sense of separate identities is present among associated Greeks which provides the basis for communication, but there is neither the isolation apparently prevalent among Americans nor the businesslike relations sometimes found among persons of the same family. M.M. was surprised by the experience of meeting a college girl whose father supported her in college but who intended to repay her father for his expenses. The businesslike arrangement between the father and daughter would be strange to the Greeks.

Another phrase used by M.M. to indicate the constellation of beliefs which surprised him about American life is the remark, "I will type it for you." Here again, there is the emphasis on the separateness of two persons. The word which accomplishes the separation is "for" — indicating the recipient of the act. M.M. rephrases the sentence to highlight the act rather than the relationship of the two people to it. He says, "I will you type it." He realizes that the sentence is not good English usage, but he shows a feeling for style in moving the word "you" forward. The early position of the word in the sentence reduces the emphasis on "done for someone else" to focus on "the act." The change strips "you" of the salience which English preserves for the sentence's last word.

A final aspect of the self which M.M. has noticed is its use of the possessive, in the sense of "drinking my coffee," "my house," and "my reaction." To him it seems that it is only the association with things or acts in the world which endows the self with significance, as though the self exists locked in solitude and requires the external world to give it vibrance and meaning. This outlook in American culture M.M. explains historically. He does not trace it back step-by-step, but instead employs a historical reserve of meaning.

The origins of the self-concept appear in the period of the Kelts in England, who "loved life but were not afraid of death." The Kelts, around 300 B.C., living in solitude on their island, were posed with the metaphysical problem of touching, the act of reaching out and embracing life and fate. Influenced by their environment, as are all people, the Kelts were pushed to an ultimate solitude in which they loved life but at the same time also embraced fate or death. By understanding and accepting fate, their life was endowed with existential beauty which is symbolized by the selection of the head of Apollo, the god of beauty, to adorn the first coin minted in England.

The capital "I" reminds M.M. of the historical heritage of the "self" concept as it originated with the Kelts. It symbolizes the subjectivity and the isolation of the self. In American culture today, however, there no longer survives acceptance of fate as the Kelts understood it.

The historical derivation of the self-concept is not in accordance with an American's understanding of a historical process. It seems symbolic and much more in the spirit of what has been called historical reserve of meaning. Past events are used in a non-historical sense, what M.M. calls suprahistorical, referring more accurately to a style of rhetoric or symbolism than to a chain of causes and effects leading from the past to the present. Concepts of beauty, freedom and the self are suprahistorical. They remain true, affect and yet remain unaffected by events which can be defined according to time or place or whether they precede or follow. M.M. finds the suprahistorical in concepts of the self and beauty among the Kelts which he perceives to cause the historical event: the minting of the coin adorned by the head of Apollo, and, eventually, the development of the capital pronoun. The self, abstract and suprahistorical, becomes historical, as an individual deriving duties and rights from the state. For M.M., the chief associations of the self are with "supraindividual," "living externally," and "power." A broad interpretation of power as behavior at the level of politics and the state reconciles the self with the state and with its association to power. M.M. says that among Greeks persons are perceived to have a self determined by the political state to which they belong. There is an understanding and a unity among Greeks, even without communication or exchange, which is derived from the recognition of a common heritage. The state is a key concept for identity and action. M.M. asserts that for him and for Greeks, morality is not a matter of religion but is based on the state.

In addition to the suprahistorical and the historical dimensions, there is the ahistorical, which refers to "absolute individual acts" (i.e., isolated acts) which are not known at the time of occurrence and, hence, are not incorporated into the body of social knowledge as cause, effect, or contingency. In the explanation of the capital self, it is obvious that M.M. turns to the suprahistorical for explanation and employs what we have called a historical reserve of meaning or a history of ideas which disregards sequence of events. The contemporary American practice of the capital pronoun is easily associated with the independent and isolated self, originating in the antiquity of England. This suprahistorical idea is given a historical expression when the head of Apollo is chosen to adorn the first coin minted by the Kelts. This event is couched in symbol and history rather than dressed in the matter-of-fact working of the American mind. Certainly there are associated with the self many historical acts but these are private and isolated and, hence, do not contribute to the concept of the self which is supraindividual and suprahistorical. This denied quality of the concept is precisely the one which for Americans is the essence of the self.

3. FORM OF ACTIVITY AND THIRD CULTURE

The American assumptions and values associated with "doing" may have both advantages and disadvantages for advisors working overseas where the valued form of activity differs from their own. Americans can find courses of action where none have been perceived before; conversely, the American's desire to move and move quickly may be very upsetting to his counterparts. Advisors have reported counterparts who were shunted aside or in some other way effectively removed from important positions because they initiated action and thereby violated the values of their own society and organization. Unlike American leaders, leaders in ascriptive societies are not expected to take action and to exercise their influence. Their function is to maintain the status quo and what they do is entrench themselves in their positions. They are usually not rewarded for initiating change and achieving progress; these are American ideas associated with achievement and action.

When Americans go overseas as advisors the temptation to get something done frequently becomes so strong that they disregard their advisory roles and attempt to do the job themselves. In Laos, for instance, the military advisors frequently resorted to giving the training themselves rather than fulfilling their mission of teaching Laotian trainers. In the Philippines, Peace Corps volunteers whose mission was to train teachers reacted in a similar manner. The Filipino teachers resented being observed by others while teaching in their classrooms and, when the Volunteers taught the classes, the Filipino teachers left the classrooms. Finally, the Volunteers themselves took over the classes for three or four months, though they ultimately realized that their approach was not very satisfactory, recognizing that the American values of "efficiency" and "time consciousness" were a hindrance to cooperation. They also mentioned that "when a problem came up, it was the American who immediately decided what to do about it. The Filipinos made no effort to do anything about a problem they might have, outside of mentioning it." The Americans added that they felt they took action primarily "because of the great difficulties involved in the Filipinos doing anything about it."* The objective of training teachers was subverted.

This frequent reaction of the overseas American advisor — doing the job himself — reflects both the form of activity of doing and the self as the responsible party. If he rejects these, accepting the norms of his counterparts and the local culture, he vitiates the reasons for his own presence. Presumably he is there because he is both an American and an expert; he has needed knowledge, skills and attitudes which his counterpart does not have. If the American acts within his appropriate frame of reference, "doing," and pushes through with his own ideas, he may alienate his counterparts and the local people; and, even if by dint of his personality and efforts the advisor completes his task, its success may not "take" in the local culture and his accomplishments may be nullified once he leaves. This latter possibility apparently is often not appreciated by Americans who strive for a quick-impact project and attempt to complete something before their tour overseas is finished. They fail adequately to integrate their work into the social structure and neglect the cultural customs and traditions needed for the success of even such simple changes (from the American point of view) as the introduction of sanitary toilets or a more effective technique of farming. Most Americans seem predisposed to believe that the desirability of the innovations they advocate is self-evident; hence, they feel their efforts will inevitably be crowned with success.

The most effective approach for the American advisor is still a matter of conjecture. He should have an understanding of both the foreign culture, the **first** culture, and of his own, the **second** culture. But his work will be carried out in the milieu of a **third** culture, which is

> created, shared and learned by men of different societies who are in the process of relating their societies, or sections thereof, to each other (Useem, **et al.**, 1963, 169-179).

John and Ruth Useem and John Donoghue in "Men in the Middle of the Third Culture point out that from the continued interaction of American advisors and their counterparts, there emerges a culture which is different from either the first or the second. Certain **themes** are characteristic of the third culture (Useem, **et al.**, 1963, 171). It is assumed that the relationship between the members of the two societies, as well as the two societies themselves, should

---

*Paraphrasing by the interviewer of a verbal report of a Volunteer.

be **coordinate**. They often are not, but the ideal is still present and its violation indicates areas of conflict between the advisor and his counterpart.

Programs sponsored in the third culture are considered to be **rational**, **secular** and **future-oriented**. Expected to show concrete results, they are construed as a beginning and are expected to grow and perhaps diffuse throughout the society. Hence, they are conceived as **expansive** and **open-ended** (Useem, **et al.**, 1963, 171-172). These characteristics of programs in the third culture represent, to varying degrees, the accepted position of the counterparts occupying administrative positions. They, of course, also represent American assumptions and values. It does not follow, however, that the attitudes of administrators in the third culture were derived from American culture.

The mention of the characteristics of the third culture must remain tentative.

> We have but dim understanding of the realities facing cross-cultural programs because we are without the existing language for making meaningful summaries of that which is experienced (Useem, **et al.**, 1963, 169).

The work of Useem, Useem and Donoghue represents an insightful excursion into the precarious area of cultural differences. In emphasizing the "third culture," the advisor is warned to resist the call of rock-ribbed Americanism and, yet, avoid the temptation of "going native."

4. PREVENTING DISEASE

The American advisor abroad does not usually have a deep understanding of the cultural background of the people he is working with. Hence, in his work he often misjudges the significance of cultural values and assumptions. This failing is particularly apparent when he is trying to introduce health measures. Success in this area, strange as it may seem, requires that the advisor instill in members of the host culture subtle assumptions and values concerning the world, activity and personal relations. It is not a matter simply of introducing new facilities and procedures. Other value components may be involved as well, such as concepts of the self, the individual, and motivation. Taking these components one at a time below, they will be applied to the general problem of disease-prevention.

Americans tend to see the world in simple terms, especially in matters involving action. They tend to regard the value of health measures as self-evident or at least easily demonstrable; therefore, the average American finds it difficult to explain to others why someone should make himself sick or uncomfortable by submitting to vaccination when he is not already sick, or why a villager in the non-Western world should go to the trouble of using only clean water to prevent illness. The reasons for both the vaccine and the clean water actually reside in an ability to anticipate consequences in the future, which is an American style of thinking but certainly not universal.

Essentially, preventive measures require the individual to anticipate a future event and connect it with present conditions and actions by means of a cause-and-effect relationship. This outlook requires an orientation to the future and faith in the individual's ability to control it through measures taken in the present. The emphasis is on the future. It includes the optimistic belief that present action can change future events — typically American beliefs but not shared by persons who are oriented toward the past or present and who are fatalistic.

The particular attitude of people toward health, body and the determinants of disease is important in establishing health measures. These Western practices are firmly rooted in the concept of the body as a biological mechanism with the determinants of disease, particularly germs, seen as external causes or, as in malnutrition, unfavorable environmental conditions. Non-Western peoples have explanations for disease which are congruent with their assumptions and values. The American advisor faces a double task in health matters, as elsewhere: he must present and establish the American way and, at the same time, he must overcome some of the ways of the local people. Disease for Americans is a physical change of the biological organism (e.g., an intrusion of germs, the breakdown of the body due to cold or fatigue, or the lack of proper food). Both health and disease are states of the biological organism conceptualized as a separate entity. In other cultures these three facets are often explained by "reasons" which, in the American view, are irrational. In Ethiopia, an American reports that a sick child grinding his jaws is looked upon as a sign of the evil eye while another writer says that in a Latin American republic, symptoms of malnutrition are often ascribed to "supernatural and other causes which bear little or no resemblance to Western medical explanations" (Erasmus, 1959, 390). The clear distinction between man and nature breaks down and the materialistic explanation of disease or lack of food is likewise not accepted. A village may continue to draw water from a contaminated pond because it is the habitation of a water spirit that would be vengeful from jealousy if the people were to use another source of water. And, among some of the Arabs, it is very difficult to clean up water holes contaminated with typhoid. Clean water is not desired by the Arabs, who prefer the strong taste given to the contaminated water by the camels. The drinker presumably acquires manly qualities from it and no connection is made between water and disease — the latter, according to the Arabs, is the will of God* (Hall, 1959, 101-102).

In a subtle manner, the American ideas of a separate self, independent of and controlling material and inanimate nature, together with an optimistic anticipation of the future, furnishes the basis for health measures. These techniques may be established on the basis of other assumptions and values; most Americans follow them out of conformity and do not necessarily understand the reasons for them, but it is, in fact, these assumptions and values which go abroad with American advisors. In some cases social imitation of the American's conduct or adherence to his exhortations establishes effective preventive health measures. In these instances the American's emphasis on

---

*Hall also reports that the Arab believes it is insane to attempt to predict future events; only God knows what the future will bring.

doing things himself, coupled with his misjudgment of the importance of social organization, induces failure once he leaves the scene.

Preventive health measures in the United States are supported by specialized roles of doctors (of different specialties), nurses, public officials, and technicians and scientists of all types. These roles are unlikely to exist in the underdeveloped countries so that the American has to adapt local social organization to continue whatever health measures he has introduced. In a specific project in Laos, for instance, wells that were placed on village grounds fell into disrepair, since the villagers did not have anyone who would naturally assume responsibility for maintaining the wells. When wells were placed on the grounds of Buddhist monasteries, however, they were maintained and even improved, although the need for these wells was no greater than for those on the village grounds. The difference in results can be attributed to the organization of the monks in the Buddhist monastery, who had the roles for effectively maintaining and, in some cases, improving the wells (Arensberg and Niehoff, 1964, 112).

5. A NEW TECHNIQUE IS INTEGRATED WITH THE CULTURAL PATTERN

The cross-cultural problems met by American advisors abroad may be very similar to intracultural problems within the same country. An example from India shows how the Indian advisor introduced a new technique in agriculture despite several cultural blocks.* From the point of view of cultural assumptions and values, the example includes all of the basic components of analyzing a culture that we have covered. However, the authors of the case-study omit elements of the case of interest from the viewpoint of this report. In the discussion below, these will be emphasized.

An agricultural project introducing the new practice of green-manuring had failed to take hold in the village of Ikari. When the villagers showed no interest in plowing-under the **san** hemp for a fertilizer, the American project advisors went to the village and soon learned that the functioning village leader was not the man who held the title, but his uncle, an older man and the head of a family known for their scholarly tradition and respected for their devout religious life. The advisors were then able to approach the real rather than the nominal source of influence. The basis of leadership was different from what an American might have expected. Note that the characteristics mentioned are head of family, older than the nephew who held the title of chairman, and the tradition of a scholarly and religious family.

The advisors approached Shri Sanehi on the use of green manure for fertilizer; however, the main point was not brought up immediately. This, again, contrasts with the American directness in social interaction, particularly

---

*The source used for this case is Albert Mayer and Associates. **Pilot Project India. The Story of Rural Development at Etawah, Uttar Pradesh.** University of California Press, 1959, 207-210. The "village worker" and the Village Participation Officer are referred to as "advisor" in the text above.

when, as in the present case, both parties have "business" to conduct and meet for that purpose. Once the advisor brought up the subject of green-manuring, Shri Sanehi agreed it would be effective. He added, however, that according to the precepts of his culture, it was enough to fulfill the average needs of the family and one should not be greedy and anxious for more economic production. One of the Indian advisors, being well versed in the cultural beliefs, was able to maintain the conversation at the level of Shri Sanehi. He argued that

> ...most people in villages nowadays were not able to meet the above-mentioned obligations to the family, the self, and...religious mendi-cants. Thus, it is even more important today to produce more and green-manuring was one of the tried methods for better production. There was no harm in doing so.

In the above words, the Indian definition of the self, the relationship of the individual to others and intimations of how the individual should conduct his life are reflected. In each instance, the concepts are different from American ones. The apt attempt of the advisor to hinge the cause of green-manuring to the Brahmin's beliefs was not immediately successful. Shri Sanehi's reply indicated the Indian's values: "I consider that for human beings, righteous conduct (dharma) is vastly more important than all the wealth of the world." He hinted that green-manuring would be an impious act and, in answer to the meek inquiries of the advisor, he stated that the act of plowing-under the **san** hemp leaf and stalk, before they are ripe, is an act of violence — and nonviolence is the greatest virtue. This remark makes sense only from the point of view that nature and plants have an essence similar to humans: the definition of the world is nonmaterialistic. The advisor's answer to the Brahmin deserves full quotation:

> The (advisor) first argued that even if a plant had a soul, it was immortal and, therefore, plowing it under would be no sin; he quoted the Bhagavad-Gita extensively, but in this he was no match for the Brahmin and his village followers. However, he continued in humility to explain that the farmer's profession was sacred, but in its pursuance many violent acts had to be committed — insects and worms were killed in the process of plowing, green grasses and weeds were rooted out for the benefit of the planted crop, and the draft animals were forced to work. Yet, the farmer did many sacred acts. He fed his family and cattle, supported the temples and priests, teachers and mendicants, and performed many other acts of hospi-tality and charity. Without the violent acts necessary to grow his crop he could do none of these acts. His sins of violence were outweighed by his acts of charity. Moreover, the land was getting poorer each year because of improper manuring. If the green-manuring were done, more of the righteous acts would be possible.

The reader can judge for himself the ingenuity of the advisors in adapting the beliefs and arguments of the Brahmin to the purpose of the new technique.

From the present point of view, the case is important because it illustrates all of the components of culture which, in turn, make the case more understandable. However, two points that are only suggested, need to be brought out more fully. The manner of interpersonal relations is only very sketchily suggested. As the advisors warmed to their subject, they apparently did not always talk directly to the Brahmin, but talked or wondered aloud, about a subject, allowing the Brahmin himself to connect it with the purpose of the meeting. And, then, there is the stress on the meekness and humility of the speech of the advisors.

The definition of the self, perception of the world and the motivation components should be abundantly clear in the above case. The component of activity is not explicitly mentioned but it is apparent throughout the whole episode. The Indian does not look to the future but to traditions. He does not value doing for its own sake. Instead, he inclines toward being. And he does not have the idea of progress. All of these points give added breadth to the meaning of the episode. The arguments which Americans might be tempted to use under these circumstances: progress, better life, material benefits, greater yield — were generally avoided by the advisors. Their argument was adapted to the values of the Brahmin. They showed how his own values required that green-manuring be tried.

6. CONCLUSIONS

American advisors frequently have difficulties in communicating and cooperating with their counterparts. The obstacles to cross-cultural under-standing may be conceptualized as differences in cultural assumptions and values. From the American's point of view, his own values and assumptions prevent him from objectively perceiving and understanding the underpinnings of the behavior of his counterpart. His performance overseas would be enhanced if he understood both his own culture and that of his counterpart.

Although a cultural pattern is an integrated whole, it may be analyzed into patterns of thinking and four components: form of activity and motivation, form of relation to others, perception of the world and perception of the self. American culture was analyzed according to these factors, with attention frequently drawn to contrasting examples from other cultures.

The emphasis on American culture as well as on contrasting cultures advocated in this book is intended to achieve four objectives:

1. Establish Conceptual Cross-Cultural Bridges

The terms used in describing American culture should serve as bridges to other cultures. Although some of the cultural concepts which have been discussed in this report cannot be literally translated into other cultures, all cultures will contain patterns of thinking, assumptions, values and norms of behavior which can be classified somewhere within the scheme provided.

2. Induce An Attitude of Cultural Relevance

A cultural characteristic represents only one of a number of possible assumptions, values or norms of behavior. Other alternatives will be found in the same culture and in different cultures — the same alternatives but with a different emphasis. Thus, the American way may not necessarily be the most desirable and certainly not the normal or natural way in a given cultural context.

3. Facilitate Self-Understanding
An awareness of American culture along with contrasting examples ought to induce understanding by the individual of himself as a cultural being. He ought to be better prepared for the hardships of culture shock and frustrations common to overseas missions and to dealing with foreign nationals in this country. He ought to be more objective in appraising himself as well as in evaluating his counterparts. In particular, he ought to be better prepared to separate cultural factors from idiosyncratic ones in himself and in others.

4. Identify Facilitating and Interfering Factors
The individual should be better able to identify those specific American predispositions that usually facilitate his work with foreign counterparts, as well as those that usually handicap him.

The attainment of the four aims above ought to lead to a more objective advisor who is capable of making the necessary observations about himself and his counterpart. His cross-cultural understanding should enable him to adapt his American modes of operation to a form appropriate to the local situation. Thus, he should be able to develop guides for his own behavior, recasting desirable goals overseas and at home into realistic activities by becoming truly a master of the art of the possible.

BIBLIOGRAPHY

1. Arnheim, Rudolf. **Visual Thinking**, University of California Press, Berkeley, 1969.

2. Arensberg, Conrad M. and Niehoff, Arthur H. **Introducing Social Change**, Aldine Publishing Company, Chicago, 1964.

3. Bell, Daniel. "The Disjunction of Culture and Social Structure: Some Notes on the Meaning of Social Reality," **Daedalus**, Vol. 94, No. 1, Winter 1965, pp. 208-222.

4. Boorstin, Daniel J. **America and the Image of Europe: Reflections on American Thought**, The World Publishing Company, Cleveland, 1960.

5. Boorstin, Daniel J. **The Americans: The National Experience**, Random House, New York, 1965.

6. Brogan, Denis W. **America in the Modern World**, Rutgers University Press, New Brunswick, 1960.

7. Bross, Irwin D. **Design for Decision**, Macmillan, New York, 1953.

8. Brown, Roger. "Language and Categories," Appendix to Bruner, J.S., Goodnow, J.J. and Austin, G.A. **A Study of Thinking**, John Wiley and Sons, New York, 1956.

9. Brown, Roger. **Words and Things**, Free Press, Glencoe, 1958.

10. Bruner, J.S., Goodnow, J.J. and Austin, G.A. **A Study of Thinking**, John Wiley and Sons, New York, 1956.

11. Cleveland, Harlan, Mangone, Gerard J. and Adams, John C. **The Overseas Americans**, McGraw-Hill, New York, 1960.

12. Cohen, Morris R. **American Thought: A Critical Sketch**, Collier Books, New York, 1954.

13. Cohen, Rosalie A. "Conceptual Styles, Culture Conflict, and Nonverbal Tests of Intelligence," **American Anthropologist**, Vol. 71, No. 5, October 1969, pp. 828-856.

14. Deese, James. **The Structure of Associations in Language and Thought**, The Johns Hopkins Press, Baltimore, 1965.

15. DuBois, Cora. "The Dominant Value Profile of American Culture," **American Anthropologist**, Vol. 57, No. 6, Part 1, December 1955, pp. 1232-1239.

16. Erasmus, Charles J. "An Anthropologist Looks at Technical Assistance," in **Readings in Anthropology, Vol. II, Readings in Cultural Anthropology**, Morton H. Fried (ed.), Thomas Y. Crowell, New York, 1959, pp. 386-403.

17. Erasmus, Charles J. **Man Takes Control**, University of Minnesota Press, Minneapolis, 1961.

18. Erikson, Erik H. **Childhood and Society**, 2nd edition, W.W. Norton, New York, 1963.

19. Foster, George M. **Traditional Cultures and the Impact of Technological Change**, Harper and Row, New York, 1962.

20. Foster, George M. "Peasant Society and the Image of Limited Good," **American Anthropologist**, Vol. 67, No. 2, April 1965, pp. 293-315.

21. Fried, Morton H. (ed.). **Readings in Anthropology, Vol. II; Readings in Cultural Anthropology**, Thomas Y. Crowell, New York, 1959.

22. Gay, John and Cole, Michael. **The New Mathematics in An Old Culture**, Holt, Reinhardt and Winston, New York, 1967.

23. Geldard, Frank A. **The Human Senses**, John Wiley and Sons, New York, 1953.

24. Glenn, Edmund S. **Mind, Culture, Politics**, mimeographed, 1966.

25. Glenn, Edmund S. "Semantic Difficulties in International Communication," **ETC.**, Vol. 11, No. 3, 1954, pp. 163-180.

26. Glenn, Edmund S. "The Use of Epistemological Models in the Analysis of Cultures," **Proceedings of the VI International Congress of The Anthropological Sciences**, Musee de L'Homme, Paris, 1963.

27. Glenn, Edmund S. "The University and the Revolution: New Left or New Right?", in **The University and Revolution**, G.R. Weaver and J.H. Weaver (eds.), Prentice-Hall, New York, 1969, pp. 99-119.

28. Goodenough, Ward H. **Cooperation in Change**, Russell Sage Foundation, New York, 1963.

29. Gorer, Geoffrey. **The American People: A Study in National Character**, W.W. Norton, New York, 1948.

30. Granet, Marcel. **La Pensee Chinoise**, Editions Albin Michel, Paris, 1950.

31. Hall, Edward T. **The Silent Language**, Doubleday, New York, 1959.

32. Hall, Edward T. and Whyte, William F. "Intercultural Communication: A Guide to Men of Action," **Human Organization**, Vol. 19, No. 1, Spring 1960, pp. 5-12.

33. Helson, Harry. **Adaptation-Level Theory**, Harper & Row, New York, 1964.

34. Henry, Jules. **Culture Against Man**, Random House, New York, 1963.

35. Hsu, Francis L.K. **Americans and Chinese: Two Ways of Life**, Schuman, New York, 1953.

36. Hulse, Frederick S. "Convention and Reality in Japanese Culture," in **Japanese Character and Culture**, Bernard S. Silberman (ed.), University of Arizona Press, Tucson, Arizona, 1962, pp. 298-307.

37. Janowitz, Morris. **Sociology and the Military Establishment**, Russell Sage Foundation, New York, 1959.

38. Kaplan, Abraham. "American Ethics and Public Policy," **Daedalus**, Vol. 87, No. 2, Spring 1958, pp. 48-77.

39. Kerlinger, Fred N. "Decision-Making in Japan," **Social Forces**, No. 30, October 1951, pp. 36-41.

40. Kerlinger, Fred N. "A Critique of Three Studies of Japanese Personality," in **Japanese Character and Culture**, Bernard S. Silberman (ed.), University of Arizona Press, Tucson, Arizona, 1962, pp. 400-413.

41. Kluckhohn, Clyde. "American Culture — A General Description," in **Human Factors in Military Operations**, Richard H. Williams (ed.), Technical Memorandum ORO-T-259, Operations Research Office, The Johns Hopkins University, Chevy Chase, Maryland, 1954, pp. 94-111.

42. Kluckhohn, Clyde. "Some Aspects of American National Character," in **Human Factors in Military Operations**, Richard H. Williams (ed.), Technical Memorandum ORO-T-259, Operations Research Office, The Johns Hopkins University, Chevy Chase, Maryland, 1954, pp. 118-121.

43. Kluckhohn, Clyde. "The Evolution of Contemporary American Values," **Daedalus**, Vol. 87, No. 2, Spring 1958, pp. 78-109.

44. Kluckhohn, Clyde and Kluckhohn, Florence. "American Culture: Generalized Orientations and Class Patterns," in **Conflicts of Power in Modern Culture: Seventh Symposium**, Lyman Bryson (ed.), Harper and Bros., New York, 1947.

45. Kluckhohn, Clyde, **et al**. "Values and Value-Orientations in the Theory of Action," in **Toward a General Theory of Action**, Talcott Parsons and Edward A. Shils (eds.), Harvard University Press, Cambridge, 1951, pp. 388-433.

46. Kluckhohn, Florence R. "Some Reflections on the Nature of Cultural Integration and Change," in **Sociological Theory, Values and Sociocultural Change: Essays in Honor of P.A. Sorokin**, E.A. Tiryakian (ed.), Free Press, New York, 1963, pp. 217-247.

47. Kluckhohn, Florence R. and Strodtbeck, Fred L. **Variations in Value Orientatons**, Row, Peterson, New York, 1961.

48. Kunkel, John H. "Values and Behavior in Economic Development," **Economic Development and Cultural Change**, Vol. 13, No. 3, April 1965, pp. 257-277.

49. La Barre, Weston. "Some Observations on Character Structure in the Orient: The Japanese," in **Japanese Character and Culture**, Bernard S. Silberman (ed.), The University of Arizona Press, Tucson, Arizona, 1962, pp. 325-359.

50. Leach, Edmund. "Anthropological Aspects of Language: Animal Categories and Verbal Abuse," in **New Directions in the Study of Language**, Eric H. Lenneberg (ed.), MIT Press, Cambridge, 1964.

51. Linebarger, Paul M.A. "Problems in the Utilization of Troops in Foreign Areas," in **Human Factors in Military Operations**, Richard H. Williams (ed.), Technical Memorandum ORO-T-259, Operations Research Office, The Johns Hopkins University, Chevy Chase, Maryland, 1954, pp. 381-400.

52. Lundstedt, Sven. "The Interpersonal Dimension in International Technical Assistance: Statement of a Problem," **Mental Hygiene**, Vol. 45, No. 3, July 1961, pp. 374-382.

53. McClelland, David C. **The Achieving Society**, D. Van Nostrand, Princeton, 1961.

54. Martindale, Don. **The Nature and Types of Sociological Theory**, Houghton Mifflin, Boston, 1960.

55. Maslow, Abraham H. **Toward a Psychology of Being**, D. Van Nostrand, Princeton, 1968.

56. Mayer, Albert and associates. **Pilot Project India: The Story of Rural Development at Etawah, Uttar Pradesh**, University of California Press, Berkeley, 1959.

57. Mead, Margaret. "The Application of Anthropological Techniques to Cross-National Communication," **Transactions of the New York Academy of Sciences**, Vol. 9, No. 4, February 1947, pp. 133-152.

58. Mead, Margaret. "The Factor of Culture," in **The Selection of Personnel for International Services**, Mottram Torre (ed.), Federation for Mental Health, Geneva, pp. 3-22.

59. Mead, Margaret. **And Keep Your Powder Dry**, William Morrow, New York, 1965.

60. Nakamura, Hajime. **Ways of Thinking of Eastern Peoples: India-China-Tibet-Japan**, East-West Center Press, Honolulu, 1964.

61. Niehoff, Arthur H. "Theravada Buddhism: A Vehicle for Technical Change," **Human Organization**, Vol. 23, No. 2, Summer 1964, pp. 108-112.

62. Northrop, F.S.C. **The Meeting of East and West, An Inquiry Concerning World Understanding**, Macmillan, New York, 1946.

63. Perry, Ralph B. **Characteristically American**, Alfred A. Knopf, New York, 1949.

64. Potter, David. M. **People of Plenty: Economic Abundance and the American Character**, The University of Chicago Press, Chicago, 1954.

65. Pye, Lucian W. **Politics, Personality, and Nation Building: Burma's Search for Identity**, Yale University Press, New Haven, 1962.

66. Ravenholt, Albert. "Feud among the Red Mandarins," **American Universities Field Staff Reports Service, East Asia Series**, Vol. XI, No. 2, 1964, pp. 175-184.

67. Reichel-Dolmatoff, Gerardo and Alicia. **The People of Aritama: The Cultural Personality of A Colombian Mestizo Village**, The University of Chicago Press, Chicago, 1961.

68. Reston, James. "Washington: on Tweedledum and Tweedledee," **The New York Times**, November 7, 1965.

69. Rogers, Carl H. "Toward A Modern Approach to Values," **Journal of Abnormal and Social Psychology**, Vol. 68, No. 2, 1964, pp. 160-167.

70. Scheler, Max. **Ressentiment**, Free Press, Glencoe, 1961.

71. Steinberg, Rafael. "Olympics Only One Star Turn," **Washington Post**, June 7, 1964.

72. Stouffer, Samuel A., **et al. The American Soldier**, Princeton University Press, Princeton, 1949.

73. Tsunoda, Ryusaku, **et al. Sources of Japanese Tradition**, Colombia University Press, New York, 1958.

74. Tung-sun, Chang. "A Chinese Philosopher's Theory of Knowledge," **ETC., A Review of General Semantics**, Vol. IX, No. 3, 1962, pp. 203-226.

75. Useem, John, Useem, Ruth and Donoghue, John. "Men in the Middle of the Third Culture: The Roles of American and Non-Western People in Cross Cultural Administration," **Human Organization**, Vol. 22, No. 3, Fall 1963, pp. 169-179.

76. Wallace, Anthony F.C. **Culture and Personality**, Random House, New York, 1961.

77. Wax, Rosalie H. and Thomas, Robert K. "American Indians and White People," **Phylon**, Vol. 22, No. 4, Winter 1961, pp. 305-317.

78. Williams, Richard H. **Human Factors in Military Operations**, Technical Memorandum ORO-T-259, Operations Research Office, The Johns Hopkins University, Chevy Chase, Maryland, 1954.

79. Williams, Robin M., Jr. **American Society: A Sociological Interpretation**, Alfred A. Knopf, New York, 1961, pp. 415-426.

80. Williams, Robin M., Jr. "American Society in Transition: Trends and Emerging Developments in Social and Cultural Systems," in **Our Changing Rural Society: Perspectives and Trends**, James H. Copp (ed.), Iowa State University Press, Ames, 1964, pp. 3-38.

81. Wittfogel, Karl A. **Oriental Despotism: A Comparative Study of Total Power**, Yale University Press, New Haven, 1957.

82. Woodard, James W. "The Role of Fictions in Cultural Organization," **Transactions of the New York Academy of Sciences**, Series II, Vol. 6, No. 8, June 1944, pp. 311-344.

INDEX